P9-CAJ-276

Essential Elements of Sustainable Urban Districts

# GRID / STREET / PLACE

*Nathan Cherry, AICP, with Kurt Nagle*

American Planning Association
**Planners Press**

*Making Great Communities Happen*

Chicago | Washington, D.C.

First published in the USA in 2009 by
**AMERICAN PLANNING ASSOCIATION PLANNERS PRESS**
122 S. Michigan Ave., Suite 1600, Chicago, IL 60603
1776 Massachusetts Ave., NW, Suite 400, Washington, DC 20036
www.planning.org/plannerspress

ISBN - 978-1-932364-72-9 (hardcover)
ISBN - 978-1-932364-71-2 (paperback)
Library of Congress Control Number 2009924832
Printed in the United States of America

All rights reserved.

© **2009 by the AMERICAN PLANNING ASSOCIATION and RTKL ASSOCIATES INC.**

**CONTRIBUTORS**

Alice Ockleshaw
Alyce Sparkman
Cody Clark
Crissy Zhou
Dave Kermode
Jenny Zhou
Johan Roa
Katie Sprague
Kelly Farrell

Nasim Yalpani
Nick Gotthardt
Orlando Sanabria
Ricardo Cervantes
Rocio Vidal
Seetha Raghupathy
Steve Knudsen
Thom McKay
Victoria Mendez

# ACKNOWLEDGMENTS

This book started as a list of questions. We had great conviction about the root premise of promoting sustainable urbanism in our practice—namely, that it is far better to promote a diversity of uses, small blocks, and compact, multifunctional open spaces in our projects than sprawl. An informal evaluation revealed that some urban districts seemed to work better than others—we wanted to know more about why.

"Formulas" for success are popular in the urban-design industry, but without our own empirical data on the subject, we could not really draw our own conclusions and "learn" with any conviction. What this research required was a significant commitment from RTKL, a firm for whom I have worked since the early 1990s. Bob Smith—who led the West Coast office of the Planning and Urban Design Group with passion, inspiration, and vision for more than 25 years—began the germination of the best practices in this book with his early use of comparable projects and research as a tool to inform the design process. Lance Josal, director of the Commercial Group, Greg Yager, director of the Planning and Urban Design Group, and Katie Sprague, director of the Branding and Environmental Graphics Group, were enthusiastic and supportive advocates from the book's inception.

The sheer amount of work required to create a book of this type—the research, drawing, writing, editing, graphic design, and marketing—required a significant team of collaborators. Sincere appreciation goes to team members Crissy Zhou, Dave Kermode, Jenny Zhou, Johan Roa, Kelly Farrell, Nasim Yalpani, Nick Gotthardt, Orlando Sanabria, Ricardo Cervantes, Seetha Raghupathy, Steve Knudsen, and Victoria Mendez, who worked creatively and with great collaborative spirit to make the first draft viable.

Throughout this process and beyond, special thanks must go to two individuals: first, Rocio Vidal, an extremely talented urban designer who worked on all aspects of the document from inception to publication—a span of two years. She directed, drew, and reviewed most of the maps and collateral information. Cody Clark, a graphic designer with exceptional talent, was most responsible for the book's overall design, and he oversaw its layout throughout. Kurt Nagle has been an essential collaborator on this project from its inception. His interpretation of what information is presented here and how helped us fundamentally with our clarity of purpose and, in the end, with the quality of the book as a whole. His wide and varied interest in great and memorable urban spaces helped direct and structure both the collection of examples and the presentation of their essential qualities. His talents as a writer helped to form and hone the observations throughout the book. He is a team member and friend of tremendous ability, humility, and collaborative spirit.

Thom McKay and Alice Ockleshaw provided much needed (and mostly gentle) in-house editorial direction. Alyce Sparkman passionately spearheaded marketing and communications. Timothy Mennel of the American Planning Association provided editorial direction to the project with pragmatism, intelligence, and a dry sense of humor. His significant input on the essay greatly strengthened its message.

This project would not have been possible without metropolitan Los Angeles itself. It is both the dynamism and dysfunction of this city that calls forth the fundamental need to seek out, learn from, and implement progressive ideas that can capture the promise of the future. To that end, some thinkers and practitioners who embody an especially progressive and inspirational vision for the region include Bill Fain, Bill Fulton, David Martin, Eric Garcetti, Emily Gabel-Luddy, Eric Moss, Gail Goldberg, John Adams, Hank Koenig, Larry Scarpa, Linda Dishman, Mark Rios, Mia Lehrer, Thomas Cox, Thom Mayne, Richard Thompson, Ron Turner, Sam Kaplan, Scott Johnson, Steven Kanner, Stefanos Polyzoides, and Vaughan Davies.

Finally, I want to thank my wife, Melissa, for her optimism and sincere interest in the project, and my three kids—Ava, Livia, and Bianca—for whom this book was written. A vast majority of the world will live in cities by mid-century, and it is my hope that this book and others like it provide a deeper understanding of how cities can function more effectively toward a shared, more sustainable future.

# CONTENTS

# GRID / STREET / PLACE

**GREATER SEATTLE**

Bellevue Downtown Park
Olympic Sculpture Park

**PORTLAND**

Pearl District
Jamison Square
Pioneer Courthouse Square

**SF BAY AREA**

Santana Row
Sunnyvale Town Center
Union Square
Yerba Buena Gardens

Ramsay Exchange

Belmar Town Center
Riverfront Park

Country Club Plaza

State Street

**SOUTHERN CALIFORNIA**

Westwood Village
Malaga Cove
Birch Street
Americana at Brand
L.A. Live
Legacy Park
Playa Vista
Valencia Town Center
Victoria Gardens
Pershing Square
Maguire Gardens
Colorado Boulevard
Rodeo Drive
Third Street Promenade
Edgemar
The Grove
One Colorado
Via Rodeo

Kierland Commons

**DALLAS**

Highland Park Village
Addison Circle
Mockingbird Station
Southlake Town Square
Legacy Town Center

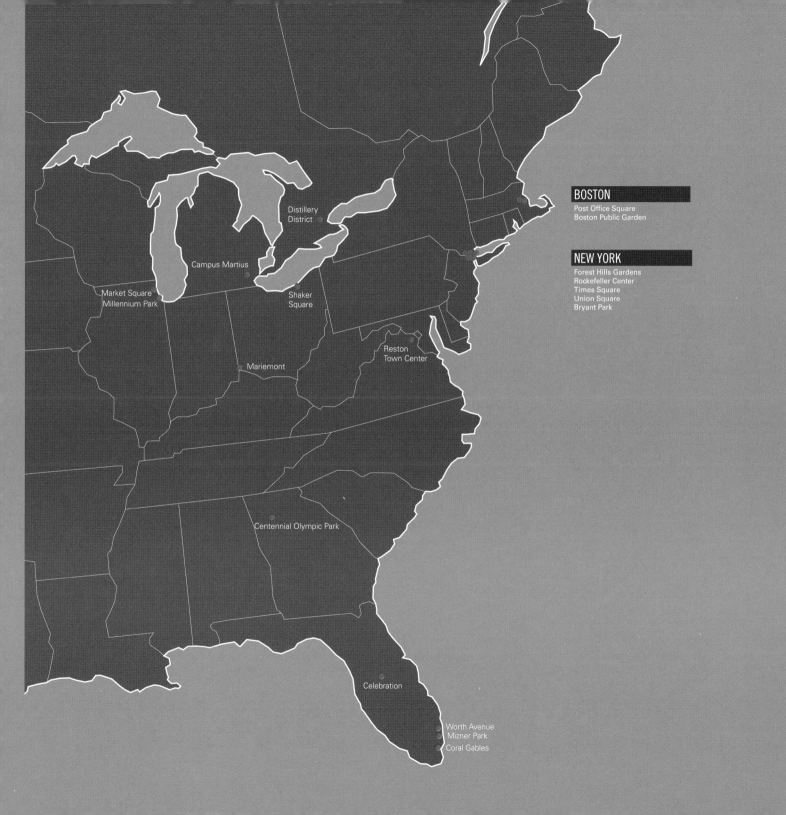

Distillery
District

Campus Martius

Market Square
Millennium Park

Shaker
Square

Mariemont

Reston
Town Center

Centennial Olympic Park

Celebration

Worth Avenue
Mizner Park

Coral Gables

**BOSTON**
Post Office Square
Boston Public Garden

**NEW YORK**
Forest Hills Gardens
Rockefeller Center
Times Square
Union Square
Bryant Park

# INTRODUCTION

In the realm of planning and urban design, three major trends have substantially influenced the public mind-set over the past decade: demographic shifts in the marketplace, ease of access to information, and concern for the environment. Taken together, these developments indicate the emergence of a more enlightened urban dweller—one who is seeking a more flexible, sustainable environment that enables a unique, diverse, vibrant, and responsible way of life. These new urbanites want an alternative to the typical postwar development patterns of suburban and semiurban sprawl.

Many of our nation's metropolitan areas have rediscovered and revitalized their urban cores, especially during these last two decades. Meanwhile, exurban growth appears to be rapidly approaching its physical limits. We are all too aware of the negative outcomes accompanying boundless urban expansion: sprawl, traffic congestion, and environmental degradation. Today, inner-ring suburbs and municipalities offer a tremendous opportunity for urban growth and renewal. They are armed with an unprecedented understanding of the need to compete with other locales and to stimulate investment in their communities by creating exciting and unique places in which to live. These places are looking for potent qualities that will distinguish them in the marketplace. Yes, they want redevelopment that is rapidly successful but increasingly they also want to be able to build a series of interrelated projects that meld organically into something more diverse and everlasting: a livable city.

Consequently, the interests of developers, the public, and municipalities are aligned more strongly now than they have ever been. How do we help all these entities get what they want? For years, we have been designing and building mixed use districts with features found in classic examples around the country. As our clients have become more informed, we have provided an expanding body of information that helps educate them about key aspects of this type of development, such as the mixture and concentration of uses, appropriate block size in the urban core, street dimensions, and the scale of public space. The more information we provide, the more engaged they become in our process. The end result, we believe, is a stronger, more cohesive design that reflects a unique collaboration and creates a place with distinct character.

This document is our "playbook"; it's the information we use to begin a design conversation with a client and other stakeholders about what a project could or should be. By gathering a range of notable projects from around North America and analyzing them in a variety of ways, we begin to understand what makes them both functionally and aesthetically successful, why they are so memorable, and, perhaps most important, why they have withstood the test of time.

We think every project in this book clearly reinforces the significance of community at three scales: grid, street, and place. Additionally, they all present a new way of thinking about sustainability—one that goes beyond green roofs and recycled materials to look at how successful places adapt and evolve over time. That said, they are definitely not the only examples of community-oriented spaces in America. Rather, they are examples most often referenced by planners, architects, and designers because they are perceived as reproducible in the marketplace and have currency in being so well known. They are a reflection of contemporary practice as much as they are a reflection of successful planning.

The result of this research has been a fascinating discovery of the remarkably universal elements of sustainable urbanism that unite even places that are strongly culturally distinct from one another. But this is just the beginning. We hope that this book can act as a template for future explorations in the realm of urban design. Most of all, we hope this book sparks discussion about its conclusions and encourages further conversation about the critical ingredients of sustainable urbanism.

*Nathan Cherry, AICP*
*Vice President, RTKL Associates*

# ESSAY
## Building the Legible City

Most American suburbs are based on an unsustainable and disorienting model of development. Ever-spreading metropolitan areas are inefficient and environmentally unsound. They are also illegible in that they lack the identity, rhythm, and structure that make them easily navigable and coherent within a larger regional context. But as Kevin Lynch—one of the guiding spirits of this project—has written, legibility works on many levels: individual understanding of a place and its functions needs to be as transparent as broader social and regional legibility.

So how do we achieve a more sustainable, balanced, and distinctive metropolis that works on all scales, from individual to regional? What are the possibilities for a more legible and viable urban future in what we've already built? One answer is that planners must tackle the dual challenge of combating urban sprawl while reinvesting in downtowns.

A brief examination of the history of suburban development in the United States helps us understand why. Americans have always been somewhat ambivalent about their cities. For much of U.S. history, rural areas have been valued for their independence, individualism, and democratic character. In sharp contrast, city centers have been associated with vast income inequality and corruption propping up political and economic elites. This image of the city—the overcrowded, unclean, and sometimes dangerous metropolis that proliferated after the Industrial Revolution—became the target of a reform movement that advocated housing bylaws and zoning restrictions to regulate growth and improve urban neighborhoods. This, however, did not prevent many from leaving the city center altogether, when they had the chance.

*The First Wave - Classic Districts and City Centers* (figure 1)

By the late 19th century, rapid expansion of transportation infrastructure— both rail service and roads—extended the distance urban workers could live from the city core, accelerating outlying development. In the early 20th century, prominent landscape architects such as Frederick Law Olmsted Jr. and John Nolen saw an opportunity in this expansion to marry suburban ideals with creative land-use planning as a means toward social reform. First-wave developments, such as Forest Hills Gardens in New York City and Shaker Heights near Cleveland, lured many city residents with hope for a better life.

Most of these experiments in community building were based on idealistic European precedents, like those of the Garden City movement, and they often delivered on their promise of a more comfortable alternative to life in the city center. Some of their best features include their walkable scale, more diverse housing stocks, moderate building density, distinct cores encompassing a compact mix of integrated land uses, well-designed and accessible outdoor spaces, and the conspicuous presence of civic buildings. However, these communities did not turn their backs on downtown, or at least not entirely. They were still tied to a city center that provided most of the jobs for their residents. Major civic and cultural institutions and the best shopping remained downtown. While offering an attractive style of home life and enough public amenities to foster community, this first wave of suburban development never posed a serious threat to downtowns as hubs of commerce and culture. At the city scale, early suburbs were part of a distinctly legible, hierarchical urban structure that had a strong, functioning downtown at its core.

**figure 1**

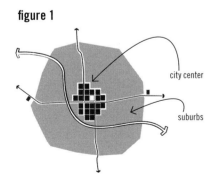

city center

suburbs

*The Second Wave - Postwar Boom and Suburban Sprawl*                    *(figure 2)*

After World War II, the spread of automobile use, freeway development, and suburban tract housing allowed more people to move away from city centers to pursue a certain strain of the American Dream, epitomized at that time by a single-family home on a quiet residential street. Commercial, industrial, and civic activities also migrated to the suburbs. Local units of government multiplied as a consequence of this growth, and they were soon in direct competition with one another to attract major employers and large, commercial, tax-generating enterprises, such as national retailers and auto malls, to expand local revenue and fund essential services. This agenda was often pursued without adequate accommodation of other land uses critical to a well-balanced community, such as affordable housing.

Downtown areas were not exempt from this competition and were often at a severe disadvantage. Eventually, major commercial and employment centers emerged throughout metropolitan regions to create our familiar multinodal urban pattern. Downtown disinvestment, growing imbalances between the number of jobs and the amount of housing in an area, the increasing prevalence of suburb-to-suburb commutes, and the seemingly endless expansion of commercial corridors came to typify the American metropolis in the postwar era.

As development boomed, the traditional urban structure dissipated into suburban sprawl, resulting in extreme auto dependency. For most Americans, cars are now the sole means of navigating this flattened, illegible metropolis. Many commutes and daily trips to run basic errands now take hours. However, the negative effects of a suburban lifestyle have become clear: a decline in civic life, environmental degradation, and increasingly costly public health consequences, such as widespread adult and childhood obesity.

There are larger-scale concerns as well, such as the social effects of global capitalism. Thomas L. Friedman and others have argued that innovations in communications, technology, and globalized business management have been dissolving the importance of place. In this 21st-century "flatland," distance and national borders no longer constrain the growth of emerging entrepreneurial giants in places such as China and India. But is place really no longer important?

There are many indications that growing numbers of people are interested in establishing roots and building more integrated lives, not just globally competitive careers and supply chains. In this, we have an opportunity to express and meet these desires for local connection in how we treat the physical forms of our cities and regions. It falls increasingly to planners and policy makers to promote better models of development.

*The Third Wave - Mixed Use Districts & Downtown Revitalization*                    *(figure 3)*

In recent decades, a renewed focus on place has become evident in the creation of mixed use districts across the country. These new districts incorporate many of the finest traits of first-wave suburban communities, which give them a vibrancy and urbanity that is absent from most of suburbia. This reawakening is also clear in ongoing efforts to revitalize downtowns and to support public spaces as the marrow of the city. While mixed use districts often struggle to achieve urbanism instantly, downtowns have capitalized on their established, well-known streets and collective outdoor spaces, such as squares, greens, and parks . But even this third wave of development doesn't solve our problems; from a regional perspective, it seems like a continuation of the zero-sum game between suburbs and traditional city centers, which has weakened metropolitan areas as a whole.

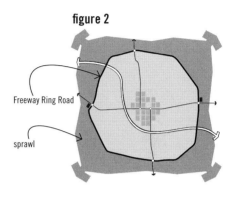

**figure 2**

Freeway Ring Road

sprawl

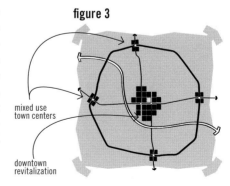

**figure 3**

mixed use town centers

downtown revitalization

*Next Wave - The Legible City*                                        *(figure 4)*

The creation of truly legible and sustainable cities requires transforming our suburbs into more livable places without abandoning downtowns. This is a regional approach that marries recent innovation with ideas and lessons from the past. For example, the value of regional open space design was apparent more than a century ago, when Frederick Law Olmsted introduced his Emerald Necklace plan in Boston and Brookline, Massachusetts. Fortunately, the value of such regional planning is again gaining currency, resulting in the creation of large public amenities. Los Angeles, for example, is currently exploring the recreational, economic, and aesthetic possibilities of its long forgotten river, which at present trickles through an unsightly concrete viaduct through the city. (Ironically, the Olmsted brothers' 1930 master plan—Parks, Playgrounds, and Beaches for the Los Angeles Region—envisioned the greening of the Los Angeles River as a key element of their grand public space concept, but was never implemented.)

*Invest in Regional Infrastructure.*

Many metropolitan areas are also realizing the importance of regional transit planning and its coordination with land-use planning and housing development. Los Angeles is now choking on traffic congestion even though it was once home to the country's most extensive metro rail network. In 2008, Los Angeles mayor Antonio Villaraigosa announced a plan to build high-density, mixed income housing along public transit corridors to revitalize neighborhoods and improve workers' mobility. Plans like these allow for more effective management of natural and man-made resources, direct growth to denser developments, and strengthen links among different parts of a region.

*Re-envision Downtown's Role.*

Regional approaches help create important environmental and transportation arteries in metropolitan areas, but they work best when they connect to a downtown that remains the beating heart of the city. Downtowns possess a tradition of public life and civic engagement that we disregard at our peril. They incubate new ideas and function like a large-scale salon, through the formal and informal relationships formed in museums, libraries, clubs, restaurants, and bars, as well as on urban campuses, plazas, and the street itself. As Richard Florida has suggested, social qualities, alongside investments in technology, can revitalize a downtown by attracting resourceful innovators who invest in it and make it competitive. By this argument, downtowns must reinvent and take advantage of their unique assets that are well-suited to the demands of the creative class and other innovative agents of business and culture. Much of the necessary infrastructure is in place to support these networks, but it is often in need of costly revitalization, restoration, and repair.

*Retool the Suburb.*

Suburban communities around the country must also fight against disinvestment. Many are doing so by capitalizing on the multinodal character of the modern metropolis and linking into built or planned regional transportation networks. Forward-looking communities are also focusing on making the most of local assets. As a result, some outlying centers of commerce are rapidly transforming into vibrant, multifunctional districts. However, a region can be weakened when suburban centers compete with a downtown for primacy. Rather, such centers are at their best when they are valuable and distinctive amenities for the community immediately surrounding them.

To become this, many successful suburban centers

- provide a broad range of activities and mixture of land uses, including residential, retail, office, civic, cultural, and open space;
- create an identifiable central district built at a higher density than the surrounding area. This density encourages a "critical mass" of businesses, institutions, amenities, and housing that sustains activity and interest in the area;

**figure 4**

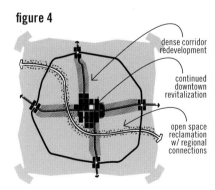

dense corridor redevelopment

continued downtown revitalization

open space reclamation w/ regional connections

- promote a diverse residential and workforce population through a variety of housing choices and workplace options;
- accommodate day-to-day needs within the district by placing personal services and convenience shopping, such as grocery and other large-format stores, within walking distance of home and work;
- link to the larger region and adjacent neighborhoods in ways that reduce reliance on cars and accommodate public transit, bicycles, and pedestrians;
- provide walkable streets that are part of a network of well-defined parks, plazas, and other outdoor spaces;
- accentuate civic and cultural spaces, particularly ones that provide essential public functions (e.g., local schools and colleges, post offices, town halls, places of worship);
- support opportunities to bring the community together through organized events in public outdoor spaces or entertainment venues (e.g., theater, cinema, restaurants, nightclubs).

Reenvisioned downtowns and retooled suburban centers are both essential components of a well-planned region, and we can create a more sustainable development model by acknowledging this. But while each area has a distinct role to play within the legible city, there are a handful of ideas that appear to underlie both.

One of these ideas is a "brand" that communicates shared aspirations and desires for the area, or its real and anticipated place in the metropolis and its history.

Unique assets make for exceptional brand stories and may provide a vital unifying concept to the district as a whole. These assets may include distinct commercial areas (such as banks, markets, and ports), well-known or established streets and public spaces, cultural or governmental institutions, sports and entertainment venues, places of higher learning and worship, and recreational areas.

However, it takes more than this to make the brand story resonate. The experience of an urban district has become less about what one does in it and more about how one feels there. This "feel" is not an easy thing to cultivate. Urban districts, both new and old, have to accommodate the dynamism of a modern, global consumer culture while remaining genuine and vernacular.

One way to do this is to take advantage of density and diversity; other development patterns cannot provide this as easily as urban districts. Close proximity among businesses, residences, institutions, and open spaces can be a boon for all involved because a unique variety of activities and services can thrive if resources are properly coordinated and shared. For example, business owners and residents can help to pay for and maintain their local parks and streets because they enjoy the park as an amenity and have a vested interest in its upkeep. Restaurants and shops can benefit from their visibility on local parks and squares. Local produce can be brought to and sold in public parks and plazas during market days, which benefits workers, residents, and local restaurants. Events that showcase local dining and other commercial establishments can be organized around major holidays in public parks or streets. There are symbiotic relationships among various elements of an urban district that, if properly coordinated, can promote a community-centered synergy.

Clearly, planning and urban design have an important role to play in creating this dynamism through the arrangement of streets and blocks, the size and configuration of open spaces, the quality of public property, streets, and passages, and the intensity and mix of land uses. Successful urban districts offer high-quality amenities through the design of their infrastructure. Sidewalks are also critical; they are not simply spaces between parked cars and destinations. In urban districts, sidewalks are vital paths between home, work, and places of rest and leisure.

There are several factors that affect their quality. One factor is the size of the urban block, which determines how one navigates through and around a district. An urban block must be small enough so pedestrians may easily traverse different neighborhoods and sections of the city, but it must be large enough to accommodate the service and parking requirements of mixed use, high-density buildings.

Another factor is how streets and sidewalks overlap in intersections. Streets must remain wide enough to accommodate traffic and the movement of goods and services, but pedestrian crosswalks must be well-designed and short enough to make crossing the street safe.

Third, the placement of utilities such as lighting is important. Sewer, water, and electrical conduits should be buried underground, preferably under parking lanes or the center of the street rather than the sidewalk. Fourth, the buildings and spaces near sidewalks must generate pedestrian activity. Shops, restaurants, and other businesses are essential in creating sidewalk traffic.

Midtown Manhattan is a prime example of a highly legible district with a strong brand story. The fact that it is a major center of fashion, publishing, and design informs how the primary public space within it, Bryant Park, works as a meeting and event space. Fashion Week, summer movies in the park, weekly tai chi classes, and free ice skating all occur in the park at different times of the year. These varied events appeal to the needs and desires of residents, workers, and visitors to the area. Equally important is the role the park plays as a daytime oasis, offering respite from the bustle of the surrounding city. On any given afternoon, there are multitudes of people quietly using the park singly or in small groups.

The brilliance of Bryant Park is that it in addition to green space, it contains food kiosks and a restaurant, providing access to a cosmopolitan marketplace while simultaneously serving as a retreat from commerce. This is reinforced at every turn and in every detail, such as the types of chairs and umbrellas in the park, the wireless Internet access, and the restaurant menus, all of which support the uniqueness of this place and its role in the city.

Without a doubt, there is a tremendous amount of time, effort, and thoughtfulness that must go into balancing the needs of the community at both the regional and local levels. But if this seems too much, planners should remember that for places to be legible, memorable, and meaningful to people—to make them care about and care for the place where they live—they must be able to bring their own perceptions and interpretations to that space, to make it their own.

Kevin Lynch, the urbanist to whom we are indebted for the concept of the legible city, writes, "The observer himself should play an active role in perceiving the world and should have a creative part in developing his image. He should have the power to change that image to fit changing needs. An environment which is ordered in precise and final detail may inhibit new patterns of activity. A landscape whose every rock tells a story may make difficult the creation of new stories."

# Smart Streets: A Critical Component of the Legible City

One of the most common challenges in urban redevelopment is how to closely structure growth that links together mixed use, transit, and open space. Mixed use creates a compact development pattern that can accommodate the greatest diversity of uses within the smallest area. Transit decouples the requirement that new development is served exclusively—or even primarily—by the automobile. Open space offers immediate pedestrian and bike access with linkages to the regional networks beyond. Transit-oriented development (TOD) offers some of the greatest promise for improving the level of sustainability for cities over the long term.

If TOD were easy, everyone would do it. The problems associated with this development pattern are numerous. Private land ownership within existing development areas makes it difficult for cities to assemble large swaths of land for redevelopment. The functioning city around these areas most often require that public rights-of-way remain at least partially functioning while the redevelopment occurs.

For many cities the greatest opportunities for TOD exist with the reconfiguration of existing auto-oriented arterials that already run through the city. This approach to accommodate transit, open space, and mixed use development with density along an established street "corridor" is an established idea that has been developed with great success in a number of cities. Examples of this type of street include St. Charles Avenue in New Orleans, Beacon Street in Boston, Avenue de la Paix in Strasbourg, France, and the Royal Parade in Melbourne, Australia.

The example illustrated here—Venice Boulevard in suburban Los Angeles—was at one time an important transit corridor linking beachside communities to downtown. In the mid 20th century, the rails were removed in the roadbed in favor of expanded travel lanes (three each way) as well as a center median for a left-turn pocket every three blocks coordinated with traffic signals. The results were to effectively change the street from a regional transit corridor that also accommodated local traffic to a regional arterial road for automobiles only. Three automobile lanes accommodate fast-moving traffic encouraged by synchronized signalization. Currently the street is quite dangerous for both automobiles and pedestrians. The left-turn pocket creates a difficult situation for oncoming traffic, ever conscious of traffic making quick left turns in front of them.

Most of the uses along the street are auto oriented, but those few pedestrians brave enough to try crossing the street are confronted with a very difficult proposition: the roadbed is over 100 feet wide and there are only a few seconds to cross the entire distance on foot.

The proposal shown here would accommodate local and regional traffic, while also reintegrating transit, expanding open space areas, adding bike access, and improving the pedestrian experience. The center median is transformed into an open space and transit corridor, eliminating left-hand turn pockets. By providing a median with transit stops in conjunction with signals every six blocks, it allows traffic to move more smoothly and safely without the danger of left-turn movements in front of oncoming traffic, and it encourages pedestrian movement along the sidewalks to the transit stops.

By expanding the tree canopy and adding lighting and signage to the sidewalks, this proposal reimagines these areas as social spaces, better able to

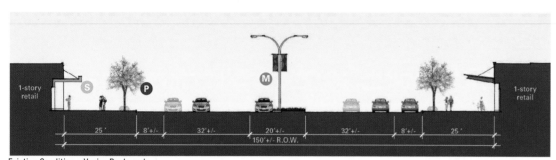

Existing Condition : Venice Boulevard

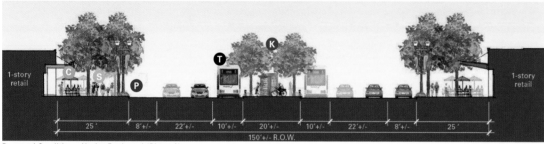

Proposed Condition : Venice Boulevard (Phase 1)

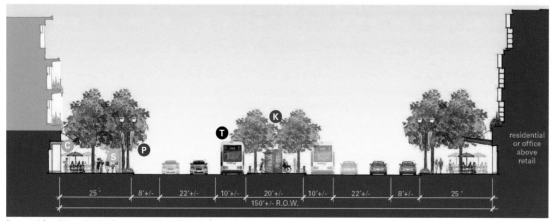

Proposed Condition : Venice Boulevard (Phase 2 Multistory Redevelopment)

accommodate outdoor activities, buffer street noise, and encourage mixed use development while also encouraging pedestrian movement. With this multimodal transportation and open space system in place at its front door, new walkable mixed use development has a tremendous locational incentive that can be further sweetened through city incentives. The city can expedite approvals for projects that have proper mix and density of uses with active pedestrian-oriented ground floors, and accommodation for transit-oriented commuter parking. The city and developers could also work in partnership to provide incentives for transit use by local businesses and residents.

The amount of traffic throughput in this example would be relatively similar to what is found along Venice Boulevard today. The reduction in traffic lights by half, the elimination of left-hand turn movements, as well as the peak demand accommodation we predict would even improve traffic circulation during key times of the day. The approach shown offers a balanced approach, where transit, bicycle, and pedestrian modes play a more integrated role in conjunction with automobiles. The street is more able to accommodate short-term traffic needs as well as future transit-oriented growth. The result is a "smarter," more sustainable urban street.

**C** Café and Outdoor seating

**K** Kiosk / Transit Lanes / Newstand / Bike Lane

**M** Center Median and Left-Turn Lane

**P** Peak: Travel Lane; Off-Peak: Parking Lane

**S** Sidewalk

**T** Transit Lane

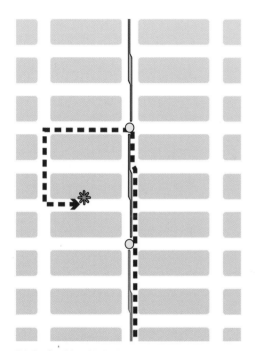

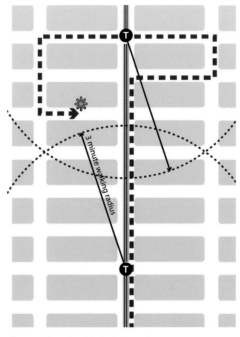

Existing Condition: Venice Boulevard

The current street configuration overemphasizes the importance of the left-turn movement and local traffic movements in general. This results in too many traffic signals and not enough capacity for regional traffic, as well as an overreliance on one transportation mode (automobile). This street condition slows down through traffic and disallows other transportation modes to be integrated into the design of the street.

Proposed Condition: Venice Boulevard

Reconfiguring the median into a transit corridor and disallowing left-hand turns allows the number of traffic signals to be reduced by half, improving the throughput capacity of the arterial road. While the street functions similarly for automobile traffic, it also now accommodates two other modes of transportation (light rail and bicycle) as well as improves pedestrian mobility in the area. Left turns require a one block rerouting to a signalized intersection, improving the safety of the movement.

○  Intersection

▪▪▶  Local Traffic Route

✳  Typical Destination

Ⓣ  Transit Lane

# CLASSIC DISTRICTS

There are a handful of well-thought-out, master planned environments around the country that have undeniably unique identities. We call them classic districts. While most have been around for many decades, they embody contemporary notions of what it is to live, work, and play. In other words, these districts have a timeless quality that makes them worthy of study. In these places, the whole is greater than the sum of its parts; they are not just collections of buildings and uses but cherished places that integrate high-quality public space with complementary architecture and landscape design.

Most of the classic districts in this book are distinctive inner-ring suburbs built in the first, second, or third decade of the 20th century for people in search of a more relaxed lifestyle and the charm of village living. Many were master planned by such luminaries as John Nolen and the Olmsted brothers. We have also included a limited number of notable, relatively new developments, such as Reston, Mizner Park, and Celebration both for the sake of comparison and because they are already regarded as new classics of community and town planning.

To help us choose and compare examples, we have identified three types of classic districts:

SHOPPING - WORKING DISTRICT: These multiuse districts are organized around a major commercial hub. Because they generate considerable regional traffic, their plans must accommodate ample parking.

TRANSIT VILLAGE: These residential districts are oriented toward transit to attract downtown commuters.

NEW COMMUNITY: These districts emphasize the public or communal nature of a development that is organized around a village core offering civic, cultural, and commercial amenities to residents.

Our study examines the patterns and relationships (to say nothing of the beauty) depicted in figure-ground diagrams created from aerial imagery. Facts and figures about each district supplement these diagrams.

# DISTRICT VIEWS

MALAGA COVE PLAZA

MARIEMONT

WESTWOOD VILLAGE

FOREST HILLS GARDENS

SHAKER SQUARE

CELEBRATION

# CLASSIC DISTRICT COMPARISON CHART

| | STREET PATTERN* | AVERAGE BLOCK SIZE | ORIENTATION TO PRIMARY STREET | CENTRAL HUB | ORIENTATION POINTS | MIXED USE | EST. GROSS FAR | LAND-USE MIX | | | |
|---|---|---|---|---|---|---|---|---|---|---|---|
| **COUNTRY CLUB PLAZA** Kansas City, Missouri | loose grid | 300' 500' 3.4 acres | parallel to primary | street | plaza + fountain | vertical | 1.5 | RETAIL | OFFICE | | |
| **HIGHLAND PARK VILLAGE** Highland Park, Texas | rectilinear grid | 130' 660' 1.9 acres | parallel to primary | paseo | fountain | vertical | 0.6 | RETAIL | OFFICE | | |
| **MIZNER PARK** Boca Raton, Florida | rectilinear grid | 300' 375' 2.6 acres | looped by primary | plaza + median | median | vertical | 1.5 | RETAIL | OFFICE | RESIDENTIAL | OTHER |
| **RESTON TOWN CENTER** Reston, Virginia | grid with arterial boundary | 270' 450' 2.8 acres | perpendicular to primary | square | fountain + square | vertical | 2.9 | RETAIL | OFFICE | RESIDENTIAL / HOTEL | |
| **STATE STREET** Santa Barbara, California | rectilinear grid | 400' 400' 3.7 acres | flanking primary | street + paseos | street | vertical | 1.3 | RETAIL | OFFICE | RESIDENTIAL | OTHER |
| **WESTWOOD VILLAGE** Los Angeles | loose grid | 350' 450' 3.6 acres | perpendicular to primary | street + squares | flatiron building | vertical | 1.6 | RETAIL | | RESIDENTIAL | OTHER |
| **WORTH AVENUE** Palm Beach, Florida | rectilinear grid | 270' 715' 4.4 acres | flanking primary | street + paseos | waterfront | horizontal | 1.1 | RETAIL | | RESIDENTIAL | |

* Shaded area connotes boundary for estimated FAR calculations.

18 Section One **Classic Districts**

| DISTRICT | STREET PATTERN* | BLOCK SIZE | ORIENTATION TO PRIMARY STREET | CENTRAL HUB | ORIENTATION POINTS | MIXED USE | EST. GROSS FAR | LAND-USE MIX |
|---|---|---|---|---|---|---|---|---|
| **FOREST HILLS GARDENS** Queens, New York | grid / organic hybrid | 230' × 600' 3.2 acres | parallel to primary | square with transit station | transit station | vertical | 1.0 | RETAIL, RESIDENTIAL, OTHER |
| **MARKET SQUARE** Lake Forest, Illinois | loose grid | 300' × 275' 1.9 acres | parallel to primary | square with transit station | transit station | horizontal | 0.7 | RETAIL, OFFICE, OTHER |
| **SHAKER SQUARE** Cleveland | loose grid | 1000' × 270' 6.2 acres | flanking primary | square with transit station | square | vertical | 1.9 | RETAIL, OFFICE, RESIDENTIAL, OTHER |
| **CELEBRATION** Celebration, Florida | radial | 350' × 400' 3.2 acres | perpendicular to primary | boulevard with canal | fountain | vertical | 1.5 | RETAIL, OFFICE, RESIDENTIAL, HOTEL, OTHER |
| **CORAL GABLES** Coral Gables, Florida | rectilinear grid | 250' × 630' 3.2 acres | flanking primary | grand boulevard | fountain | horizontal | 1.0 | RETAIL, OFFICE, RESIDENTIAL, HOTEL, OTHER |
| **MALAGA COVE** Palos Verdes Estates, California | organic | 270' × 1000' 6.2 acres | parallel to primary | plaza | fountain | horizontal | 0.7 | RETAIL, OFFICE, RESIDENTIAL, OTHER |
| **MARIEMONT** Mariemont, Ohio | radial | 250' × 660' 3.8 acres | flanking primary | square | art piece | horizontal | 0.7 | RETAIL, OFFICE, RESIDENTIAL, OTHER |

\* Shaded area connotes boundary for estimated FAR calculations.

# CLASSIC DISTRICT SCALE COMPARISON

Classic districts, despite having common elements, can differ widely in form.
Below are several classic districts at 1:1200 scale.

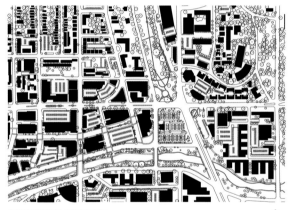

**COUNTRY CLUB PLAZA**
Kansas City, Missouri

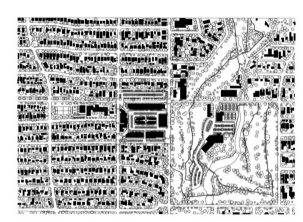

**HIGHLAND PARK VILLAGE**
Dallas

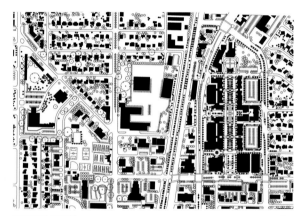

**MIZNER PARK**
Boca Raton, Florida

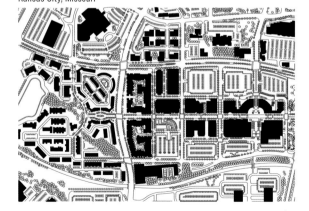

**RESTON TOWN CENTER**
Reston, Virginia

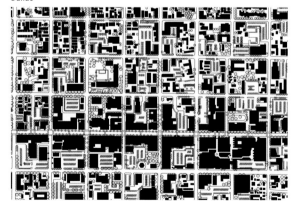

**STATE STREET**
Santa Barbara, California

**WESTWOOD VILLAGE**
Los Angeles

0'      600'
300'      1200'

**WORTH AVENUE**
Palm Beach, Florida

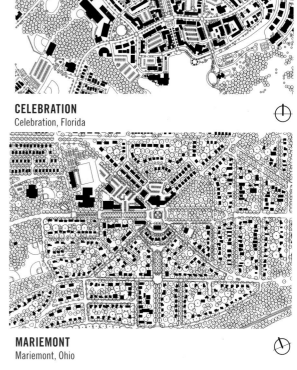

**FOREST HILLS GARDENS**
Queens, New York

**MARKET SQUARE**
Lake Forest, Illinois

**SHAKER SQUARE**
Cleveland

**CELEBRATION**
Celebration, Florida

**CORAL GABLES**
Coral Gables, Florida

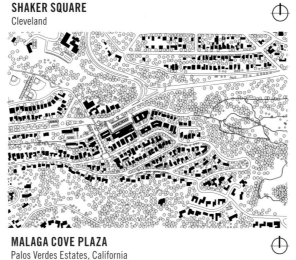

**MALAGA COVE PLAZA**
Palos Verdes Estates, California

**MARIEMONT**
Mariemont, Ohio

0'    600'
300'    1200'

# COUNTRY CLUB PLAZA

Kansas City, Missouri

A 55-acre shopping district located four miles south of downtown Kansas City, Missouri, the plaza was the first shopping center to successfully accommodate cars without compromising the pedestrian experience. The plaza was part of J. C. Nichols's vision for the Country Club district and was master planned by Edward Buehler Delk in 1922. Built in the Spanish Revival style, it expresses its European inspiration in its public spaces, architecture, and public art. Parking and access is handled inventively, with parking either concealed below

grade or above in "wrapped" structures; this leaves sidewalks and gathering spaces largely uncompromised. Today, the mix of high-end retail, restaurants, entertainment options, and offices continues to thrive, thanks to renovation and revitalization in the late 1970s

Metro Kansas City    CBD

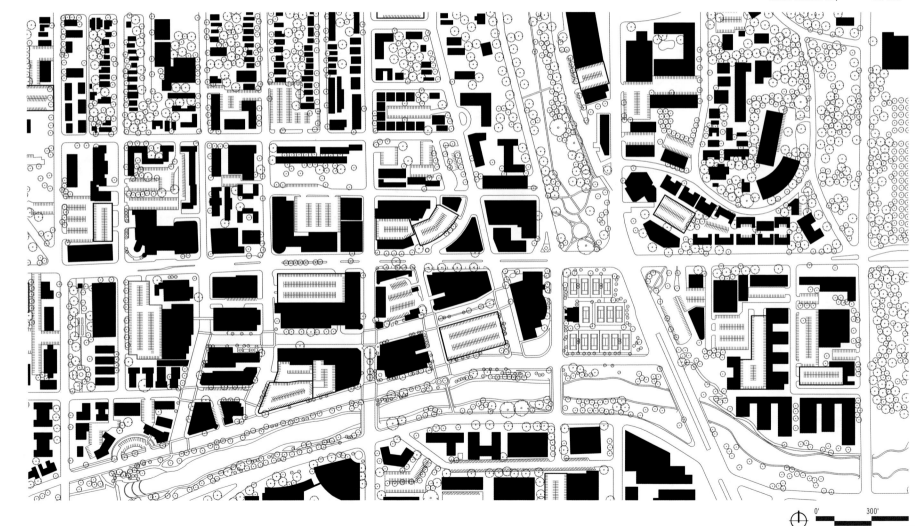

0'    300'
100'    500'

# HIGHLAND PARK VILLAGE
Dallas

Dallas's Highland Park Village was the first single-owner, private retail development that was undivided by city streets. Developers began working on the project in 1928 and employed local architectural firm Fooshee and Cheek to create a town square inspired by visits to California, Mexico, and Spain. Featuring red tile roofs, stucco and terra-cotta facades, brick paths, and a central fountain, the "Spanish village" accommodated service-oriented tenants, such as a grocery and post office, and complemented the ample parks and sophisticated aesthetic of neighboring Highland Park. Today, Highland Park Village continues to thrive with a variety of restaurants and high-end retailers.

Metro Dallas    ▨ CBD

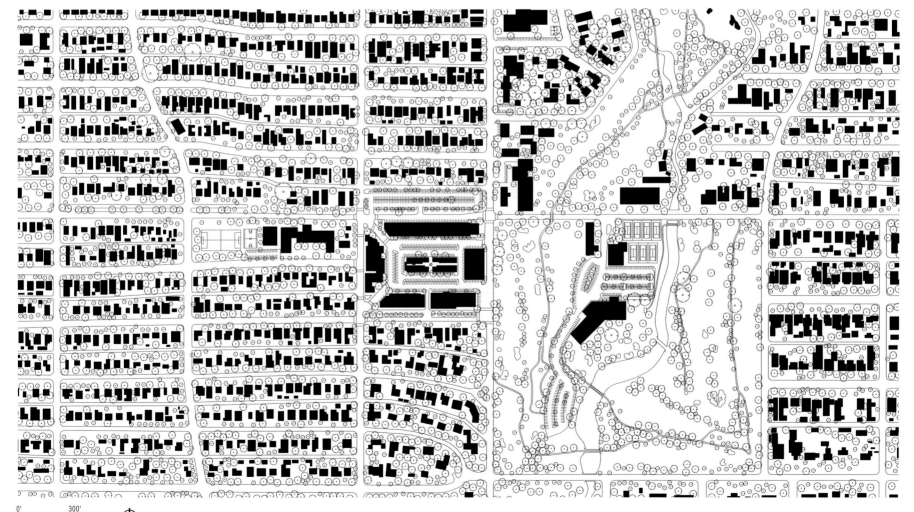

0'    300'
100'    500'

# MIZNER PARK

Boca Raton, Florida

Developed in the 1990s by Crocker and Company, Mizner Park is one of the first and most successful mixed use redevelopments of a mall site in the United States. The site was once home to the small, enclosed Boca Mall, which opened in 1974 and closed in the late 1980s because of regional competition. Mizner Park covers 30 acres of land and contains more than 40 shops and restaurants, an eight-screen cinema, 300 apartments, roughly 200,000 square feet of office space, an outdoor amphitheater, and the Boca Raton Museum of Art. The area features a wide median with interconnected retail kiosks, seating areas, fountains, and grassy play areas. One-way streets create a loop road around the central median, resulting in an unusually wide street section; roughly 200 feet lie between buildings on opposite sides of the street. The plan is notable for how it separates uses into zones: in the western part of the development, offices are built above retail spaces; residential buildings have ground-floor retail in the eastern section; cultural facilities are located on the north side; dedicated retail pad sites are located on the south side.

Metro Fort Lauderdale ▪ CBD

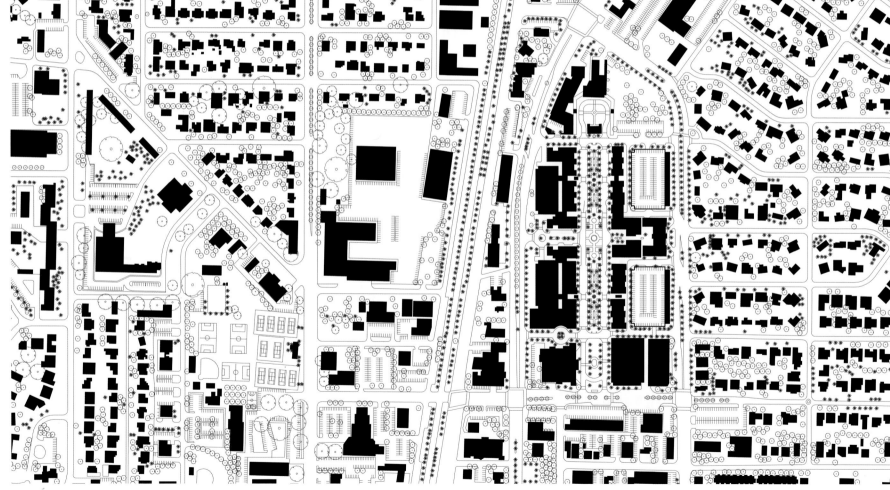

0'  100'  300'  500'

## Shopping / Working Districts
# RESTON TOWN CENTER
Reston, Virginia

With its small blocks, high-quality infrastructure, mix of uses, and events programming throughout the year, Reston draws visitors from all parts of northern Virginia. The 60-acre center's first phase was developed in the 1990s by Reston Town Center Phase I Associates and Himmel/MKDG. It included the 514-room Hyatt Regency Hotel, an 11-screen cinema, and the four buildings surrounding Fountain Square, which yield 220,000 square feet of retail space and 290,000 square feet of office space. Fountain Square is about an acre in size; its main landmark is Mercury Fountain. Directly in front of Mercury Fountain is Market Street, and across the street is the Pavilion, which operates as a covered open-air ice rink during the winter and a flexible event space the rest of the year. Later development phases expanded the office and residential components of the project.

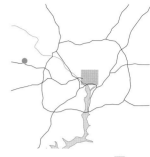

Metro Washington    CBD

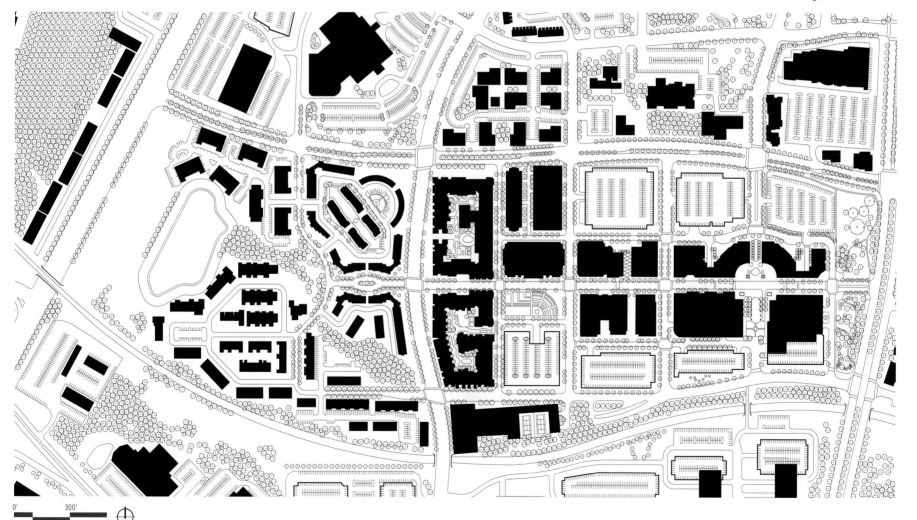

0'  100'  300'  500'

## Shopping / Working Districts
# STATE STREET
Santa Barbara, California

Santa Barbara was settled in the 17th century around one of the Spanish missions along the Camino Real. Santa Barbara's most important spine road is State Street, which starts near the ocean and heads northwest toward the original town settlement. State Street consists of a number of historic mixed use buildings, which feature ground-level, pedestrian-oriented goods and services, and office and residential space on upper stories. The street includes the Santa Barbara Museum of Art and the Public Library. The downtown blocks are large (roughly 400 by 400 feet), which creates the need for midblock

pathways for pedestrians. Three open-air shopping paseos on State Street are particularly interesting: El Paseo, La Arcada, and Paseo Nuevo. El Paseo and La Arcada were both built in the 1920s and are two of the finest early examples of open-air shopping centers in California. Of similar quality but built much later, Paseo Nuevo was completed in the mid 1990s and contains more than 50 shops, restaurants, a movie theater, and a performing arts center.

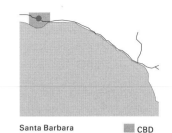

Santa Barbara ☐ CBD

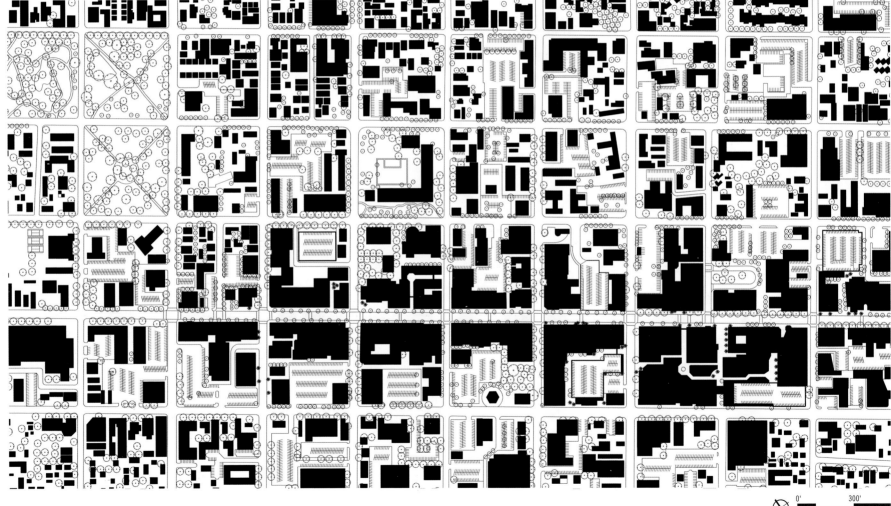

0'      300'
100'      500'

# WESTWOOD VILLAGE

Los Angeles

The Janss Investment Company created Westwood Village in the 1920s as a shopping district and corporate headquarters. Master planned by the Olmsted brothers, its idiosyncratic street pattern broke from the city grid of Los Angeles and provided a unique template for future growth. The success of the village was augmented by the rapid growth of its venerable neighbor to the north—the University of California, Los Angeles. Today, it serves both the residents of Westwood and the university. As one of the country's great college towns, the village is highly distinctive; university-related shops and services mingle with larger retailers, restaurants, and cafés. In the past, independent merchants complained about a lack of parking. However, a city-owned garage was recently constructed and now provides easy access to 24-hour parking. Westwood is also the home of the Hammer Museum, which houses renowned collections of impressionist and modern art.

Metro Los Angeles  CBD

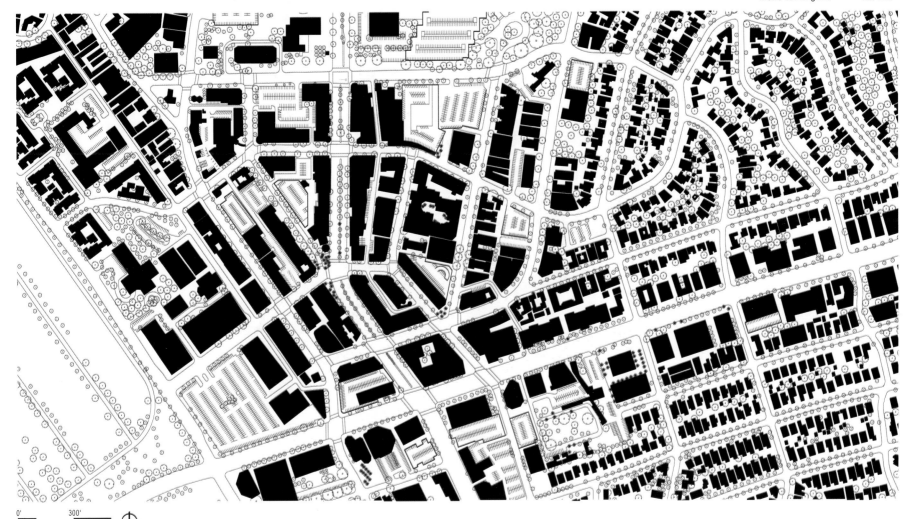

0'    300'
100'    500'

# WORTH AVENUE

Palm Beach, Florida

Worth Avenue is an upscale shopping street in Palm Beach, Florida, that stretches four blocks from Lake Worth to the Atlantic Ocean. The street first became fashionable after the construction of the Everglades Club in 1918, which was designed by Addison Mizner. The street is home to approximately 250 shops, boutiques, restaurants, and art galleries, with upper-story offices and residences. The street's unique identity is shaped by arcades that create walkways lining both sides of the street. Additionally, midblock passages (known locally as "vias") run perpendicularly from Worth Avenue; small retail and restaurants are clustered around them. The Esplanade lies at the eastern end of Worth Avenue and offers a variety of upscale shops anchored by a major department store.

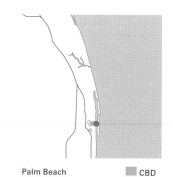

Palm Beach          ▨ CBD

0'          300'
100'          500'

# FOREST HILLS GARDENS

Queens, New York

This 6,000-resident neighborhood in the Borough of Queens, New York, was inspired by the 19th-century "Garden City" movement pioneered in communities near central London. The movement advocated self-sufficient, mixed use suburbs as an alternative to the factory towns of the time. In 1909, the Russell Sage Foundation hired landscape designer Frederick Law Olmsted Jr. and architect Grosvenor Atterbury to conduct an experiment in townmaking by blending progressive planning ideas, an elaborate landscape palette, and period architecture. Central to the plan were shops and restaurants adjacent to a Long Island Rail Road station. In order to encourage transit ridership, garages are small even by early 20th-century standards; streets allow parking for residents only. The West Side Tennis Club provides affordable recreation for residents and was home to the U.S. Open tennis championship until 1978. Today, the area contains some of the most desirable housing in Queens.

Metro New York  CBD

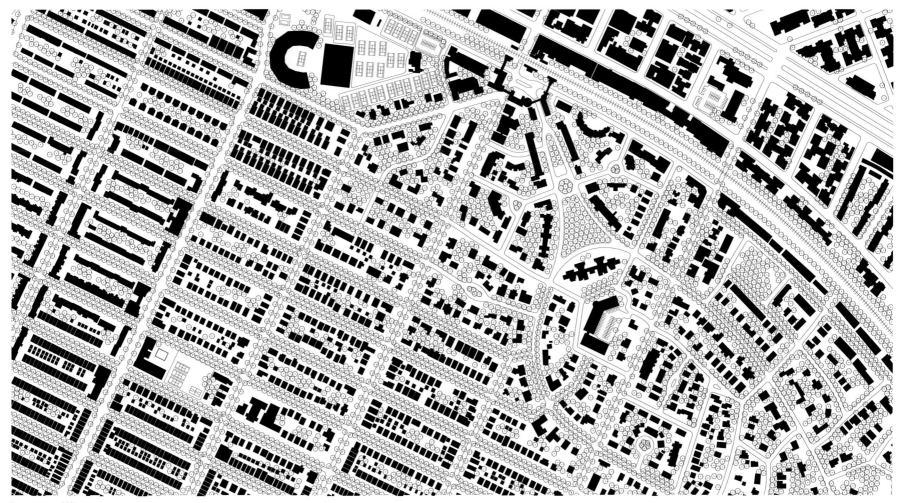

# MARKET SQUARE

Lake Forest, Illinois

Planned and designed by Howard Van Doren Shaw and completed in 1917, U-shaped Market Square surrounds a central green terminated by a train station. Market Square consists of multistory, mixed use buildings that house retail, banking, and professional services, as well as restaurants. The square was part of a visionary plan that anticipated commuter travel; the tree-lined district accommodates a parking area for commuters who take the train to and from downtown Chicago from the station on the far side of the square, thereby directing pedestrian traffic past shops and restaurants on the way to and from the station. Funded and operated through a private land trust, Market Square has become the civic heart of Lake Forest and hosts a number of annual city-wide events and celebrations. In 1978, it was listed in the National Register of Historic Places as the nation's first planned shopping center.

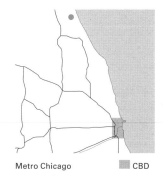

Metro Chicago      CBD

# SHAKER SQUARE

Cleveland

The gateway to the suburb of Shaker Heights, Shaker Square was one of the earliest planned transit-oriented developments in the United States. The Van Sweringen brothers built the square in the 1920s and based its central octagonal area on the famous Amalienborg Square in Copenhagen, Denmark. They also built the transit line that connects Shaker Square to downtown Cleveland. The square accommodates on-street, angled parking and provides a central gathering space lined with restaurants, galleries, shops, a six-screen movie theater, and a fitness center. Upper stories provide office space to local professionals. The American colonial- and Georgian-style architecture fits thematically with nearby residential neighborhoods. Today, the square continues to serve the surrounding community and is in the midst of world-class cultural, educational, and health-care institutions. Shaker Heights remains one of the most ethnically and socially integrated communities in the United States.

Metro Cleveland    ▨ CBD

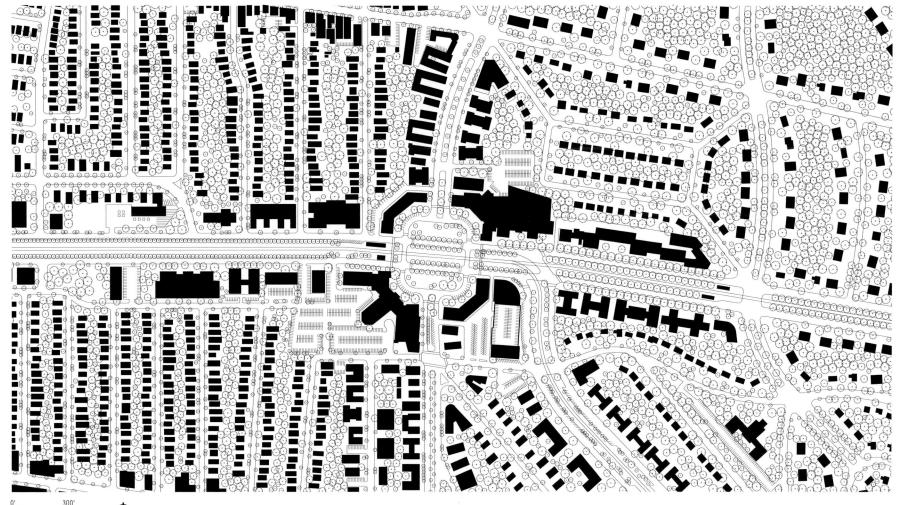

0'     300'
100'     500'

# New Communities
# CELEBRATION
Celebration, Florida

The master planned community of Celebration was conceived by the Disney Development Corporation and was built adjacent to the Walt Disney World Resort in 1996. Robert A. M. Stern and Cooper, Robertson & Partners collaborated in designing the community's master plan. The plan consists of a radial grid intersected by curvilinear arterial roadways that converge on a mixed use town center and lakefront promenade. Noted architects Michael Graves, Cesar Pelli, and Philip Johnson designed individual buildings in Celebration.

Residential structures include detached single-family homes, town homes, and flats, all of which have vehicular access to rear alleys. Celebration is often cited as a model example of new urbanism because of its robust mix of uses, pedestrian-oriented public spaces, accessible street layout, and regionally appropriate architecture.

Metro Orlando ▪ CBD

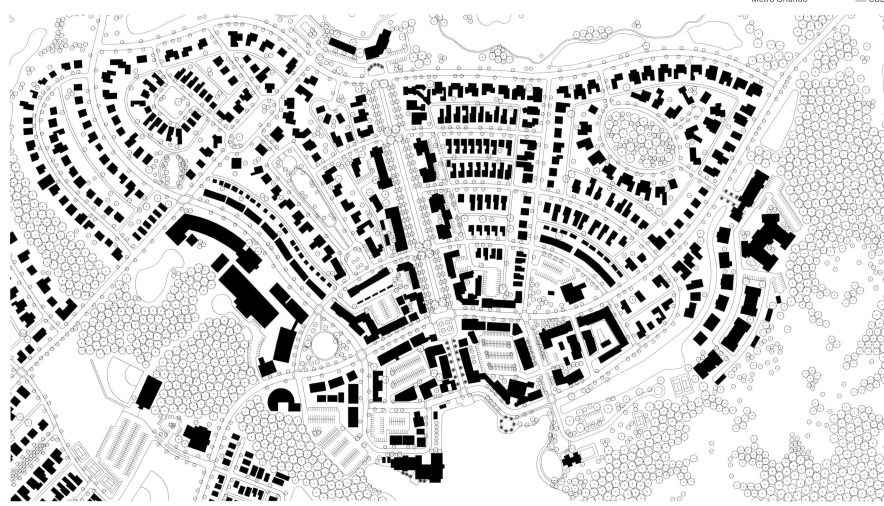

## New Communities
# CORAL GABLES
Coral Gables, Florida

Coral Gables was designed in the early 1920s according to the dominant city-planning principles of the time. Developer George Merrick created a community with wide tree-lined streets, monumental buildings, winding roadways, plazas, fountains, and ample green space. Spanish and Mediterranean Revival-style buildings are complemented by seven eclectic villages. Two of the community's standout features are the Venetian Pool, a quarry that was transformed into a lagoon, and the Biltmore Hotel, now a national historic landmark.

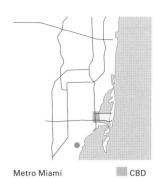

Metro Miami          CBD

0'    300'
100'    500'

## New Communities
# MALAGA COVE PLAZA
Palos Verdes Estates, California

Incorporated in 1939, the city of Palos Verdes Estates was among the first master planned communities in the United States. Malaga Cove Plaza is one of the oldest developments in the city and the only shopping district completed out of the four originally envisioned in early plans. The plaza was planned by the Olmsted brothers; the architecture was designed by Charles H. Cheney. The plaza houses the Myron Hunt–designed Palos Verdes Public Library, which was placed on the National Register of Historic Places in 1995. The plaza

features an arcade that links the buildings. Retail, office, and civic spaces ring the plaza, and a replica of Bologna's Neptune Fountain adorns its center. The buildings that surround the plaza are some of the earliest examples in California of designs that comply with a community-based design guideline. The plaza's aesthetics and architecture continue to be protected by the Art Jury, a nongovernmental organization that must approve any exterior alteration to buildings, fences, sidewalks, and other structures.

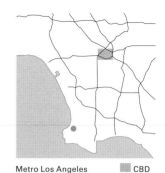

Metro Los Angeles ▪ CBD

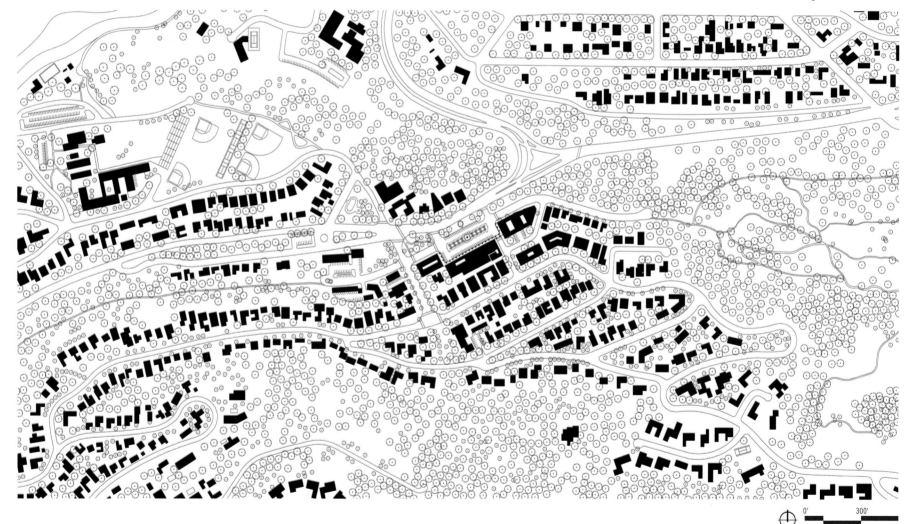

# New Communities
# MARIEMONT
Mariemont, Ohio

Mariemont is one of the first master planned new communities in the United States. It was conceived in the 1920s by philanthropist Mary Emery and landscape architect John Nolen. The village, which is approximately one square mile in size, has about 1,400 dwellings, an abundance of parks, playgrounds and playfields, and numerous shops, offices, and entertainment venues. The plan is notable for its unique radial street pattern and spine road with a grand median. Although significantly lower in density than other examples in this book, Mariemont blends town planning, landscape design, and architecture with a controlled palette of materials and textures to create a beautiful and successful community.

Metro Cincinnati    CBD

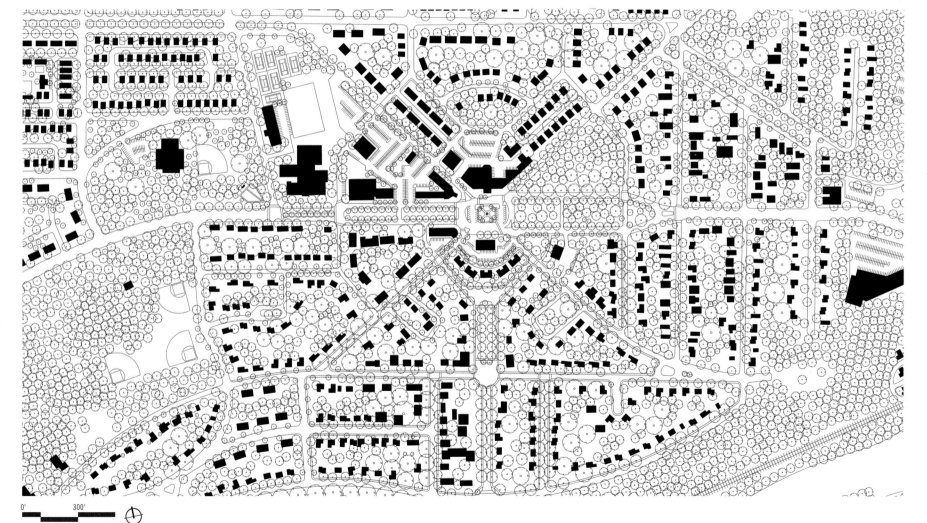

# MIXED USE DISTRICTS

Like the classic districts in the prior section, mixed use districts are singular developments that bring together a broad range of activities, including commercial, residential, and high-quality, outdoor recreational activity. However, these districts are of relatively recent origin—at least as the products of conscious planning—and frequently arise as a result of the current trend in favor of infill and transit-oriented development in urban areas.

Mixed use developments are also found outside traditional downtown centers and follow a development pattern along major highways that connect to the urban core. As such, their strength (and weakness) is that they are seen as "urban enough" for their constituency—safer, less gritty alternatives to the true, incrementally developed center city. Many mixed use centers have success providing their habitués with a convenient, safe, and clean alternative to downtown, but they have also in the process assumed some key services originally only provided by downtowns, which threatens the health of those downtowns as the vital cores of their communities. In response, traditional urban centers must accept their diminished roles as commercial retailing hubs and modify themselves to offer unique experiences that newer mixed use districts cannot provide. Further, some downtowns adopt aspects of land-use policies and values that have been developed in these mixed use centers in order to compete more directly with them. (As one example, some downtowns cultivate big-box retail by providing incentives that encourage smaller footprints with multiple stories, to better promote a dense urban setting.)

The districts featured in this section are frequently cited by design and development professionals, professional journals, and popular magazines as noteworthy or outstanding examples of contemporary community development. Not surprisingly, most of these examples are located in major growth areas, such as the San Francisco Bay Area, greater Los Angeles, and the Dallas–Fort Worth metropolitan region.

Our study focuses on key issues such as block structure, land-use mix, and open-space distribution and character. We use color-coded diagrams that depict the fundamental structures of these places to help identify differences and commonalities. The information used to prepare these diagrams was drawn from a variety of sources, including aerial imagery, site visits, photos, and Web research. Because these districts are at various stages of development, our mapping typically depicts projects at buildout; we note exceptions below.

# DISTRICT VIEWS

PLAYA VISTA

ADDISON CIRCLE

RIVERFRONT PARK

DISTILLERY DISTRICT

MOCKINGBIRD STATION

PEARL DISTRICT

# FIGURE GROUND

**THE AMERICANA AT BRAND**
Glendale, California
*Completed*

**SUNNYVALE TOWN CENTER**
Sunnyvale, California
*Planned*

**SANTANA ROW**
San Jose, California
*Completed*

**THE PEARL DISTRICT**
Portland, Oregon
*Completed*

**BIRCH STREET**
Brea, California
*Completed*

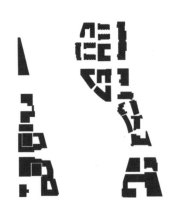

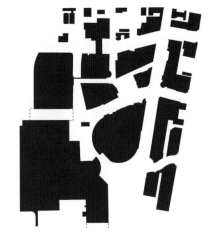

**RIVERFRONT PARK**
Denver
*Phase Two Under Construction*

**L.A. LIVE**
Los Angeles
*Phase One Under Construction*

**VALENCIA TOWN CENTER**
Valencia, California
*Completed*

0'      500'
200'      1000'

**RAMSAY EXCHANGE**
Calgary, Alberta, Canada
*Planned*

**MOCKINGBIRD STATION**
Dallas
*Completed*

**KIERLAND COMMONS**
Scottsdale, Arizona
*Completed*

**DISTILLERY DISTRICT**
Toronto, Ontario, Canada
*Completed*

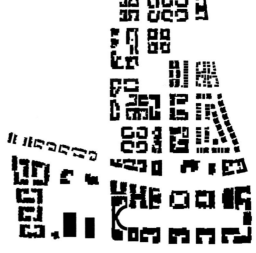

**ADDISON CIRCLE**
Addison, Texas
*Phase Two Under Construction*

**LEGACY PARK**
Tustin, California
*Planned*

**PLAYA VISTA**
Los Angeles
*Completed*

0'    500'
200'    1000'

# LAND-USE MIX

- ● Commercial (Office + Retail)
- ● Mixed Use (Residential over Retail)
- ● Hotel
- ○ Residential
- ○ Civic/Institutional

- ○ Parks and Open Space
- ○ Undeveloped Land
- ● Parking Structure
- ○ Surface Parking

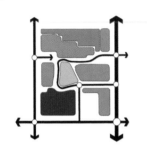

**THE AMERICANA AT BRAND**
Building Total: 1,132,000 SF
Residential: 660,000 SF
Retail + Office: 472,000 SF

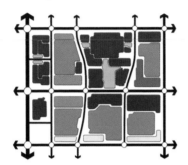

**SUNNYVALE TOWN CENTER**
Building Total: 2,061,000 SF
Residential: 501,000 SF
Retail + Office: 1,420,000 SF
Hotel: 140,000 SF

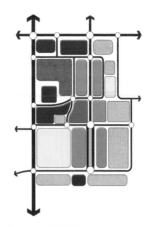

**SANTANA ROW**
Building Total: 2,035,000 SF
Residential: 1,200,000 SF
Retail + Office: 760,000 SF
Hotel: 75,000 SF

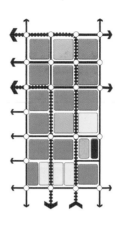

**PEARL DISTRICT**
Building Total: 3,233,000 SF
Residential: 2,975,000 SF
Retail + Office: 258,000 SF

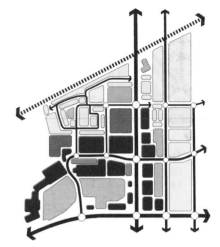

**BIRCH STREET**
Building Total: 954,000 SF
Residential: 385,000 SF
Retail + Office: 569,000 SF

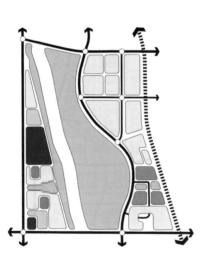

**RIVERFRONT PARK**
Building Total: 2,971,000 SF
Residential: 2,903,000 SF
Retail + Office: 68,000 SF

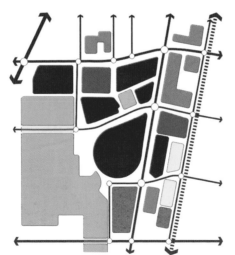

**L.A. LIVE**
Building Total: 6,445,000 SF
Residential: 2,270,000 SF
Retail + Office: 2,436,000 SF
Hotel: 1,590,000 SF
Civic: 149,000 SF

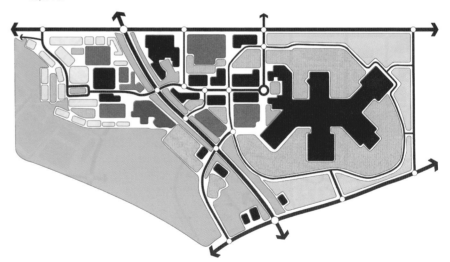

**VALENCIA TOWN CENTER**
Building Total: 2,380,000 SF
Residential: 708,000 SF
Retail + Office: 1,446,000 SF
Hotel: 226,000 SF

0'  200'  500'  1000'

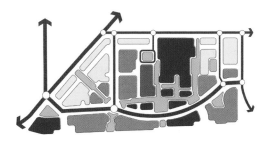

### RAMSAY EXCHANGE
Building Total: 2,562,000 SF
Residential: 1,930,000 SF
Retail + Office: 552,000 SF
Hotel: 80,000 SF

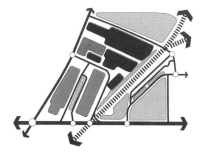

### MOCKINGBIRD STATION
Building Total: 1,146,000 SF
Residential: 236,000 SF
Retail + Office: 910,000 SF

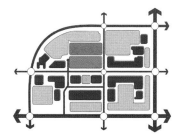

### KIERLAND COMMONS
Building Total: 850,000 SF
Residential: 350,000 SF
Retail + Office: 500,000 SF

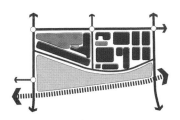

### DISTILLERY DISTRICT
Building Total: 827,000 SF
Residential: 495,000 SF
Retail + Office: 332,000 SF

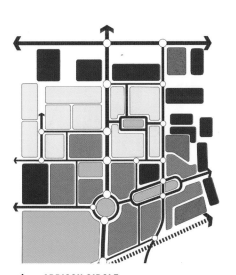

### ADDISON CIRCLE
Building Total: 3,775,000 SF
Residential: 2,540,000 SF
Retail + Office: 552,000 SF

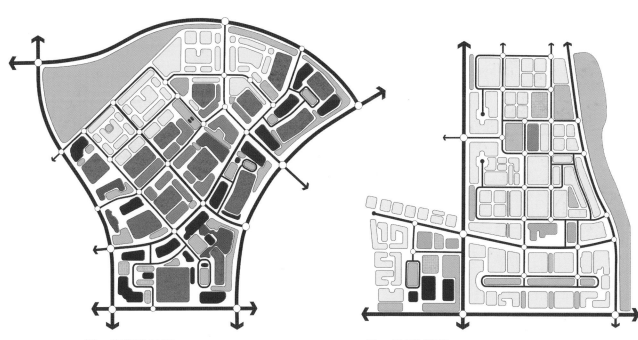

### LEGACY PARK
Building Total: 4,145,000 SF
Residential: 1,370,000 SF
Retail + Office: 2,375,000 SF
Hotel: 380,000 SF
Civic: 20,000 SF

### PLAYA VISTA
Building Total: 8,445,000 SF
Residential: 8,107,000 SF
Retail + Office: 264,000 SF
Civic: 74,000 SF

0'    500'
200'    1000'

# COMMERCIAL MIX

Legend:
- Mixed Use Commercial
- Retail
- Office
- Hotel

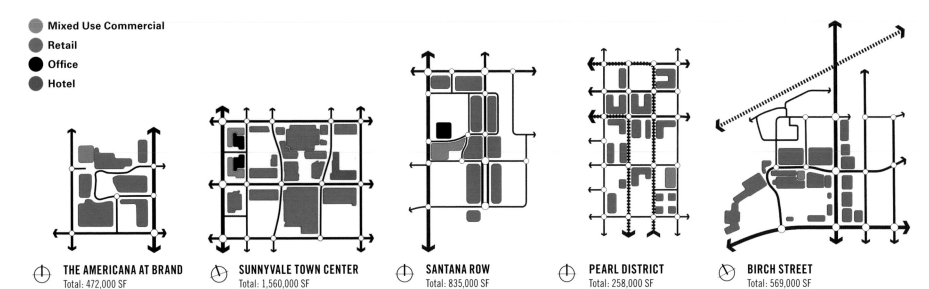

**THE AMERICANA AT BRAND**
Total: 472,000 SF

**SUNNYVALE TOWN CENTER**
Total: 1,560,000 SF

**SANTANA ROW**
Total: 835,000 SF

**PEARL DISTRICT**
Total: 258,000 SF

**BIRCH STREET**
Total: 569,000 SF

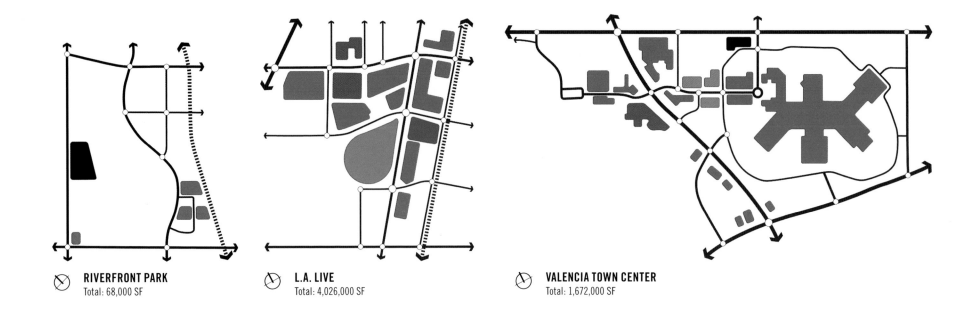

**RIVERFRONT PARK**
Total: 68,000 SF

**L.A. LIVE**
Total: 4,026,000 SF

**VALENCIA TOWN CENTER**
Total: 1,672,000 SF

0'   200'   500'   1000'

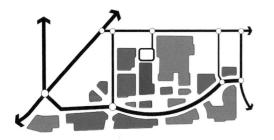

**RAMSAY EXCHANGE**
Total: 632,000 SF

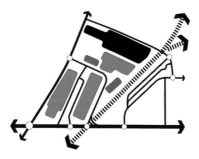

**MOCKINGBIRD STATION**
Total: 910,000 SF

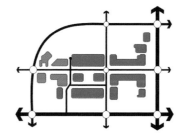

**KIERLAND COMMONS**
Total: 500,000 SF

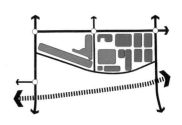

**DISTILLERY DISTRICT**
Total: 332,000 SF

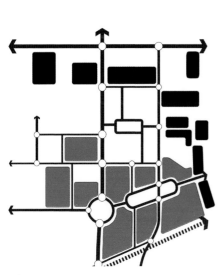

**ADDISON CIRCLE**
Total: 552,000 SF

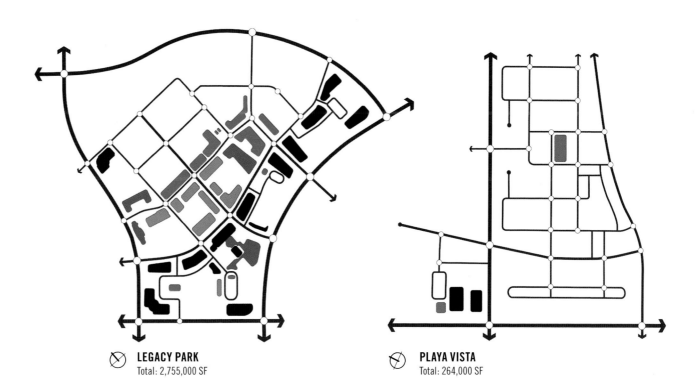

**LEGACY PARK**
Total: 2,755,000 SF

**PLAYA VISTA**
Total: 264,000 SF

0'    500'
200'    1000'

# RESIDENTIAL MIX

- Single Family Residential
- Townhouse
- Apartment (rental product)
- Condo / Flat (owner product)
- Loft / Live-Work

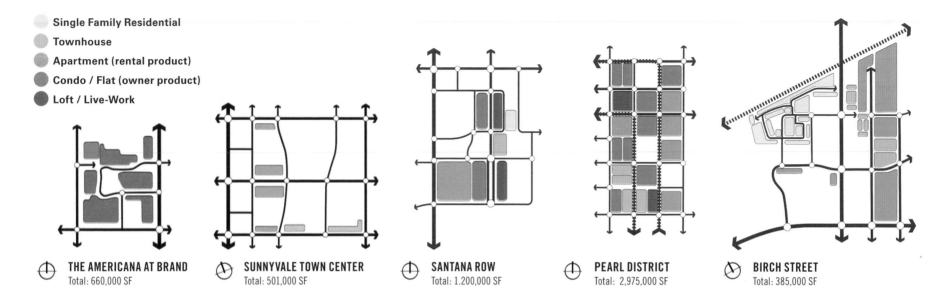

**THE AMERICANA AT BRAND**
Total: 660,000 SF

**SUNNYVALE TOWN CENTER**
Total: 501,000 SF

**SANTANA ROW**
Total: 1.200,000 SF

**PEARL DISTRICT**
Total: 2,975,000 SF

**BIRCH STREET**
Total: 385,000 SF

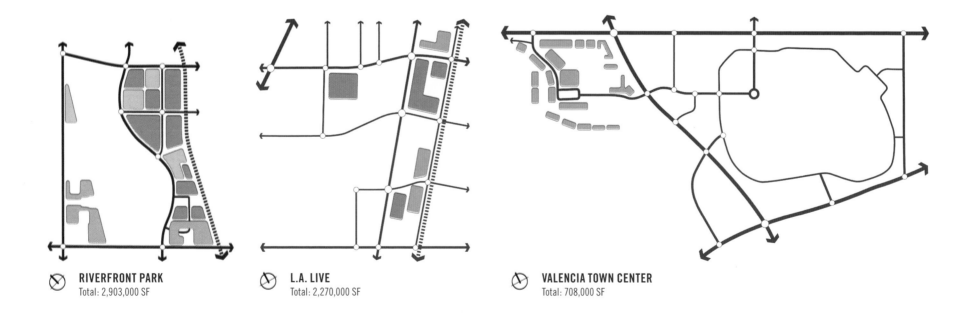

**RIVERFRONT PARK**
Total: 2,903,000 SF

**L.A. LIVE**
Total: 2,270,000 SF

**VALENCIA TOWN CENTER**
Total: 708,000 SF

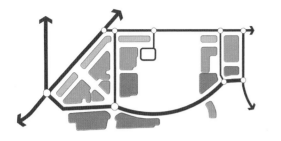

⊕ **RAMSAY**
Total: 1,930,000 SF

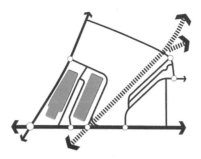

⊕ **MOCKINGBIRD STATION**
Total: 236,000 SF

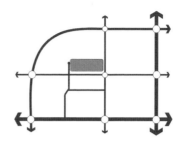

⊕ **KIERLAND COMMONS**
Total: 350,000 SF

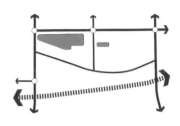

⊕ **DISTILLERY DISTRICT**
Total: 495,000 SF

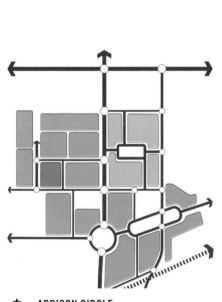

⊕ **ADDISON CIRCLE**
Total: 2,540,000 SF

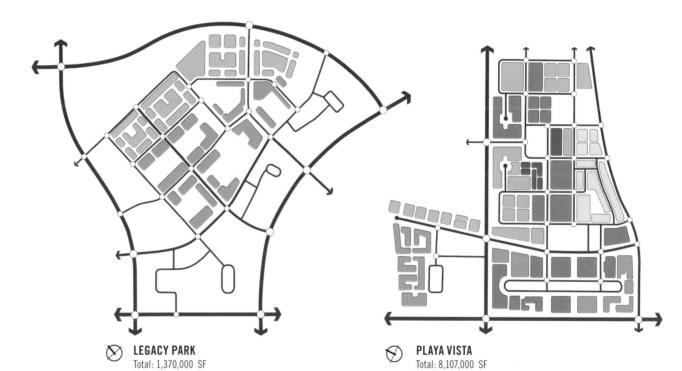

⊘ **LEGACY PARK**
Total: 1,370,000 SF

⊘ **PLAYA VISTA**
Total: 8,107,000 SF

# OPEN SPACE NETWORK

Passage
Park
Streetscape
Square / Event Space
Water Body
Undeveloped

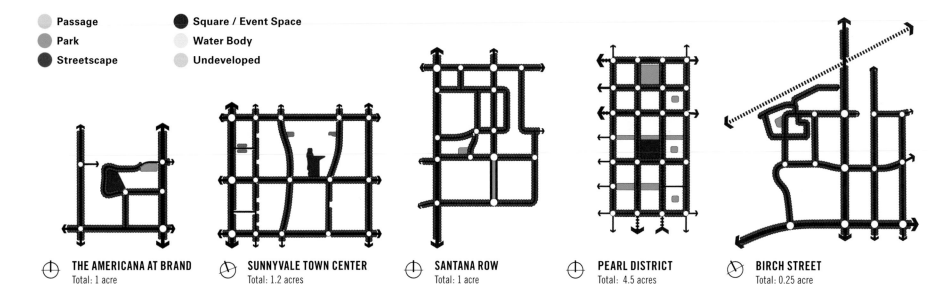

**THE AMERICANA AT BRAND**
Total: 1 acre

**SUNNYVALE TOWN CENTER**
Total: 1.2 acres

**SANTANA ROW**
Total: 1 acre

**PEARL DISTRICT**
Total: 4.5 acres

**BIRCH STREET**
Total: 0.25 acre

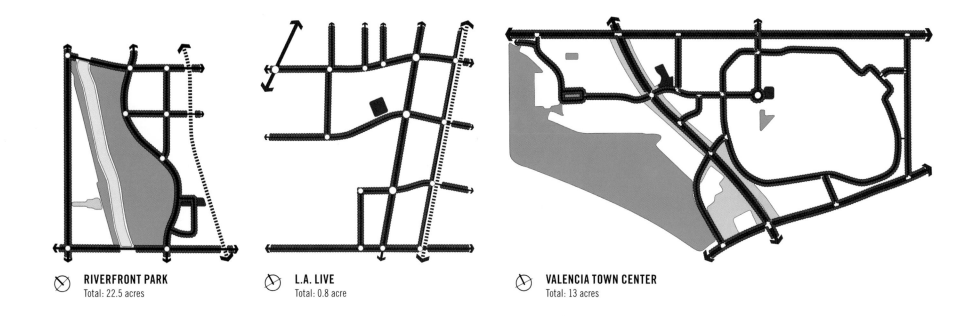

**RIVERFRONT PARK**
Total: 22.5 acres

**L.A. LIVE**
Total: 0.8 acre

**VALENCIA TOWN CENTER**
Total: 13 acres

0'    500'
200'    1000'

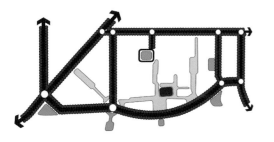

⊕ **RAMSAY EXCHANGE**
Total: 3.5 acres

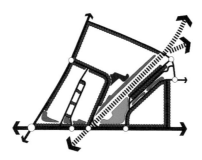

⊕ **MOCKINGBIRD STATION**
Total: 3 acres

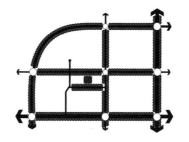

⊕ **KIERLAND COMMONS**
Total: 0.5 acre

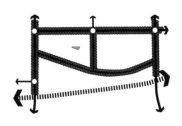

⊕ **DISTILLERY DISTRICT**
Total: 0.1 acre

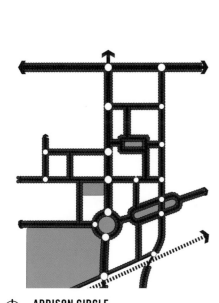

⊕ **ADDISON CIRCLE**
Total: 24 acres

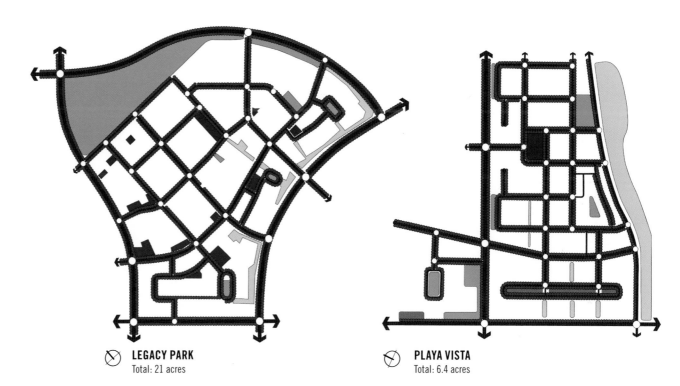

⊘ **LEGACY PARK**
Total: 21 acres

⊘ **PLAYA VISTA**
Total: 6.4 acres

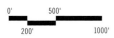

# PROJECT LAND AREA

The amount of land area covered by a project is a strong indicator of its location within a metropolitan region. Among the projects we studied, the smaller sites (such as Ramsay and the Pearl District) tend to be denser developments in or around the urban core that take advantage of access to public infrastructure, such as transit and open-space amenities. Projects with larger land area (such as Legacy Park and Valencia Town Center) are often regional destinations serving growth beyond the inner ring of the urban core.

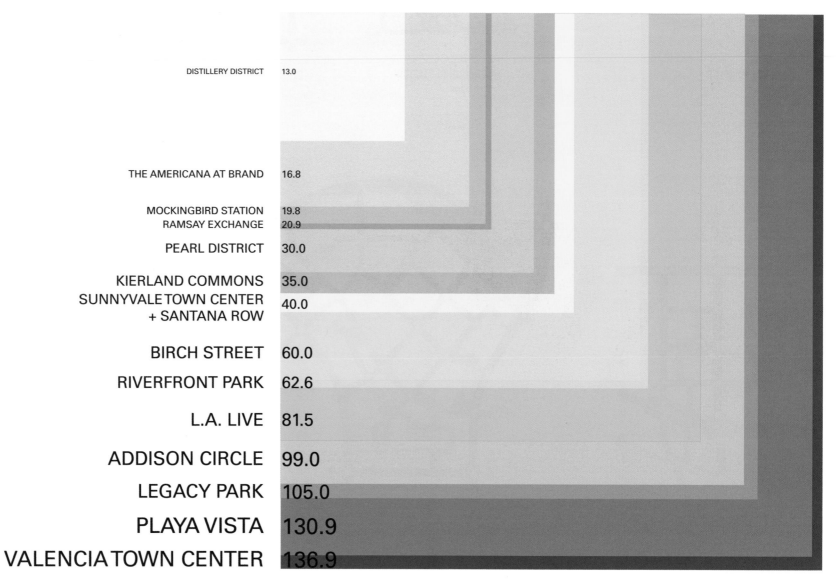

| | |
|---|---|
| DISTILLERY DISTRICT | 13.0 |
| THE AMERICANA AT BRAND | 16.8 |
| MOCKINGBIRD STATION | 19.8 |
| RAMSAY EXCHANGE | 20.9 |
| PEARL DISTRICT | 30.0 |
| KIERLAND COMMONS | 35.0 |
| SUNNYVALE TOWN CENTER + SANTANA ROW | 40.0 |
| BIRCH STREET | 60.0 |
| RIVERFRONT PARK | 62.6 |
| L.A. LIVE | 81.5 |
| ADDISON CIRCLE | 99.0 |
| LEGACY PARK | 105.0 |
| PLAYA VISTA | 130.9 |
| VALENCIA TOWN CENTER | 136.9 |

0'      200'

100'      400'

# LAND USE BY PERCENTAGE

There is considerable variation among the examples in how many square feet they devote to retail, office, hotel, civic, and residential land uses. Nonetheless, some trends are clear. All of the projects (except for Riverfront Park) include residential, retail, and office space, although the precise mixture varies; some projects emphasize their residential function, whereas others are more clearly shopping or employment destinations. The examples show that residences are an essential component of successful mixed use space. Residential uses are rarely less than 30 percent of the total project area in sustainable mixed use districts. The amount of space devoted to housing is often much higher because major traffic and parking challenges are relatively easy to solve

with respect to how housing functions with other uses. The amount of office use also varies a great deal—some projects, such as Mockingbird Station, take advantage of nearby transit service to become significant centers of employment. Mostly one must understand the impact that retail has on general district functions. It is preferable for retail space to account for a relatively minor percentage of overall land use—providing basic services to people who live or work locally, as in the Pearl District and Addison Circle. However, when retail space functions as a regional shopping attraction, taking up anywhere from 35 to 50 percent of a development's footprint (as in Valencia Town Center, Sunnyvale, and Americana at Brand), there are "spikes" of activity through the day—some at lunchtime but mostly during prime after-work shopping hours and on weekends. The traffic accommodations for these times tend to have negative impacts—making streets wider, walking areas narrower. Additional traffic movements created by regional retail also negatively affect air and noise quality within the urban district as well.

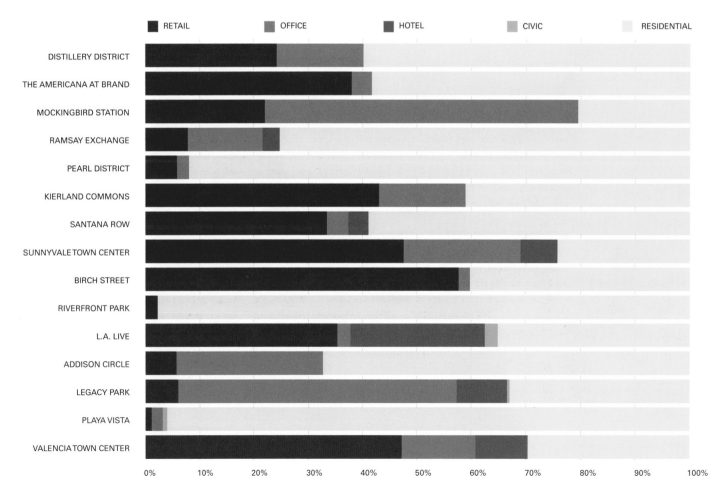

# LAND COVERAGE BY ACREAGE

Although there is great variability in terms of project size, this graph suggests there is a proportional relationship among the amounts of land devoted to buildings, streets, and open spaces. For example, open space rarely makes up more than 40 percent of the overall land area in these projects, and it is typically about the same size as the building footprint. In fact, the most prevalent designs show an "equal thirds" balance of buildings, streets and surface parking, and open space. These relationships become clearer in the next graph, depicting land coverage by percentage.

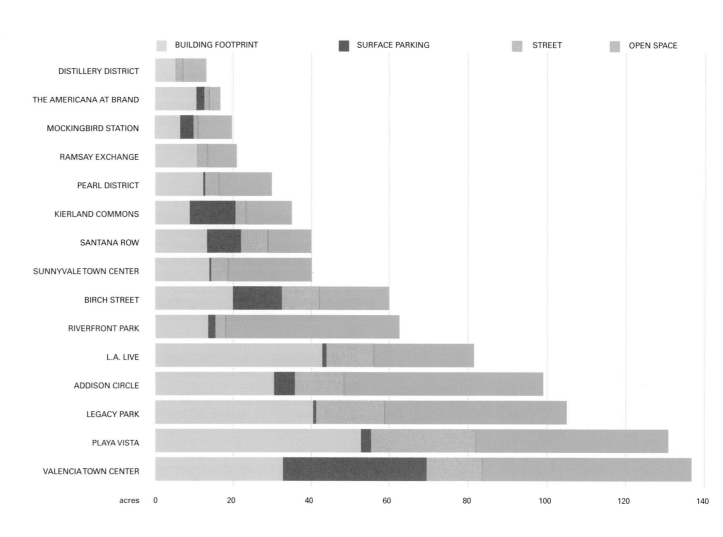

BUILDING FOOTPRINT    SURFACE PARKING    STREET    OPEN SPACE

DISTILLERY DISTRICT
THE AMERICANA AT BRAND
MOCKINGBIRD STATION
RAMSAY EXCHANGE
PEARL DISTRICT
KIERLAND COMMONS
SANTANA ROW
SUNNYVALE TOWN CENTER
BIRCH STREET
RIVERFRONT PARK
L.A. LIVE
ADDISON CIRCLE
LEGACY PARK
PLAYA VISTA
VALENCIA TOWN CENTER

acres    0    20    40    60    80    100    120    140

# LAND COVERAGE BY PERCENTAGE

The percentage of land area devoted to buildings, streets, and open space is fairly consistent across projects, especially when the two most extreme examples are eliminated. (Americana at Brand has an unusually high building coverage of 60 percent; Riverfront Park is approximately 75 percent open space.) We found that streets consistently take up between 15 and 25 percent of the development area. Surface parking is the least consistent land-cover variable among the examples because it reflects differences in development intensity (conveyed by surface parking versus structured parking). Building coverage typically ranges from 25 to 45 percent, and 20 to 40 percent of a site is devoted to open space. Not surprisingly, the lowest percentages for building coverage tend to be found in the projects that are farthest from the urban core, mostly because of the significant space requirements for surface parking.

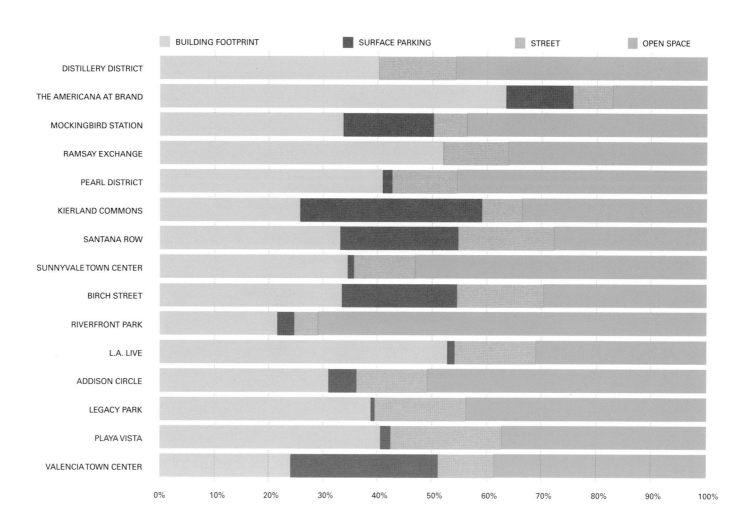

# PROJECT INTENSITY (FAR)

Variation in project intensity is a reflection of comparative land value and proximity to the core, both of which also influence the relative compactness of the project area. Projects that achieve a gross floor area ratio (FAR) over 1.0 seem to achieve a functional threshold or critical mass at which significant pedestrian activity and viable mixed uses support each other better in conjunction with reasonable traffic flows than those at lower density. L.A. Live and the Pearl District in Portland are good examples of "downtown adjacent"

mixed use districts. Those projects with lower FARs are generally located in outlying suburban communities and emphasize regional retail over a more integrated or balanced mix of uses (see Valencia Town Center and Kierland Commons).

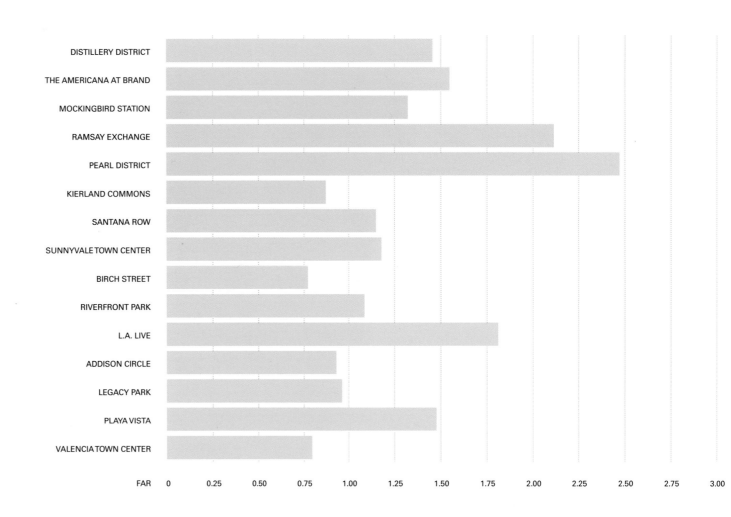

# GROSS DWELLING DENSITY (DU / ACRE)

Dwelling densities range from less than five dwelling units per gross acre to more than 50. The lowest densities are typically found in outlying developments that function as regional commercial centers, such as Valencia Town Center and Kierland Commons. The highest dwelling densities are found in compact developments located near the urban core, such as the Pearl District and Ramsay. Our experience of these places suggests that a minimum of 10 dwelling units per gross acre is necessary to achieve a sustained level of pedestrian activity and an active street life within mixed use environments. The type and diversity of housing product is also an important consideration when assessing the character and function of each district. Moderate density developments (e.g., Addison Circle, Riverfront Park, and Playa Vista) rely on buildings that are between three and five stories tall to incorporate significant residential development. Higher-density projects (e.g., the Distillery District, the Pearl District, and Ramsay) mix medium-profile urban blocks with high-rise towers (15 to 35 stories) at key locations.

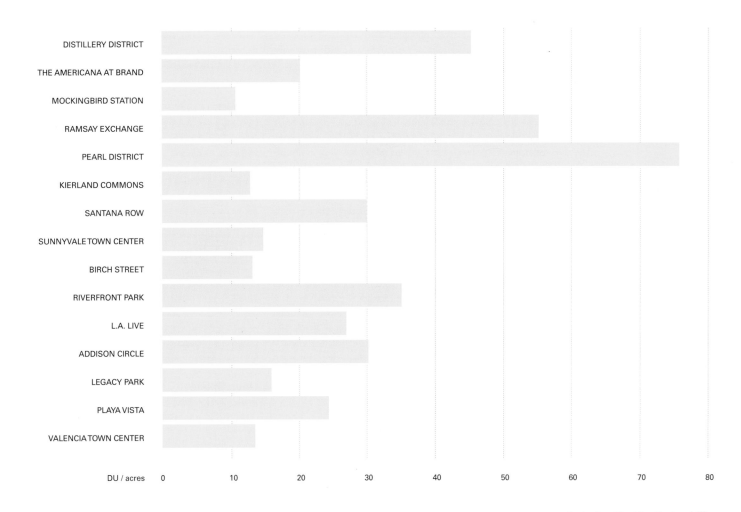

## Discrete Size

Most examples in this chapter range in size from 25 to 50 acres of completed development within five to 15 years of groundbreaking. A few examples, such as Valencia, Addison, and the Pearl District, are larger but have been phased in, with a portion of the development core completed early on to create a central activity hub and project identity.

## Access

The projects are often near or adjacent to major arterial streets that have four to six lanes of two-way traffic. Within the projects themselves, the streets tend to be gridded and narrower: double two-way travel lanes on the busiest streets, two single travel lanes for local streets. Shopping streets rely on slow-moving, compactly spaced traffic flows, centrally located parking, and pedestrian activity, and not high speed traffic.

## Block Structure

Block dimensions range from 200-by-200 feet (the Pearl District) to 600-by-400 feet (the Distillery District). While it is hard to say what a "typical" block dimension is, widths between 300 and 400 feet tend to be the most flexible. This dimension allows a pedestrian to walk one side of the block in roughly a minute and a half, which is reasonable for pedestrian activity, yet is also wide enough for phased development to occur flexibly. An urban block should be able to accommodate early development of a single-story use with surface parking behind it, as well as more intensive uses, such as above-grade parking structures wrapped with mixed use buildings, street-oriented ground floors, and high-activity sidewalks.

## Density

In construction up to four or five stories, net density typically ranges from 1.0 to 1.5. Structured parking is a necessity, which tends to expand the block dimension. A much more transit-oriented FAR is usually 2.0–3.0, with transit access immediately adjacent to the core, but this relies on greater-density buildings of typically five to eight stories. Examples with denser FARs (4.0 and above) are best incorporated as small infill clusters within the core of an urban district. Towers of 15 to 25 stories can be integrated well if planned with special consideration for shadowing, glare, and access, among other issues.

## Land-Use Mix

The districts studied here are most often a mix of residential, retail, office, civic, and hotel uses within a compact area. The core of the district should integrate mixed uses and have a strong, definitional vertical presence. The more integrated and varied the land use is in a development, the more inviting it is as a walkable mixed use environment. Our examples were one of three types of land-use mix: balanced mixed use (roughly equal amounts retail/office-hotel/residential, as in Mockingbird Station, L.A. Live, and Legacy Park); residential-driven mixed use (Pearl District, Riverfront Park, and Playa Vista); and retail-driven mixed use (Valencia, Kierland Commons, Birch Street, and Sunnyvale). The balanced and residential-driven mixed use projects tend to have more constant activity through a longer portion of the day and night, with fewer "single purpose" traffic movements.

## Retail Footprint

The retail footprint of districts that mostly serve local residents is generally between 50,000 and 250,000 gross square feet (Distillery District, Addison Circle, Playa Vista). They are often a mix of smaller shops, convenience retail, and restaurants, which are frequented by local residents and tend to generate more pedestrian activity on the street than large anchor retail. Regional centers are roughly between 500,000 and 2 million gross square feet (Americana at Brand, Sunnyvale, Santana Row, Birch Street). A mix of retail tenants from local, regional, and national brands is common.

## Office Mix

Office space in the districts seems to have three thresholds: less than 100,000 gross square feet (GSF) (Riverfront Park, Birch Street, Americana at Brand); 250,000 to 500,000 GSF (Mockingbird Station, Ramsay Exchange, Addison Circle, Sunnyvale); and more than 500,000 GSF (Legacy Park, L.A. Live). Three types of office space seem to be especially important to an urban district's success: "Class A" space, which is characterized by a large floor plate with 25,000 to 30,000 GSF per floor; creative office space, which contains loftlike, narrower office space above retail; and live/work space, which is typically an on-street office space with living space above it. The mix of office types helps attract a wider array of businesses and workers to the development.

## Residential Mix

Most districts in this chapter have a variety of private and rental properties, housing types, and price points. The most successful examples integrate an assortment of different types of urban residences, such as lofts, town houses, and live/work units. Some of these units need to be directly accessible from the street, as this creates more pedestrian activity in the district. For residential space to make an impact on mixed use districts, there must be at least 100 units on a site, or 25 percent of overall net land use devoted to housing. The example with the most residences is the Pearl District, which has more than 6,000 housing units—amounting to 90 percent of the district's land use.

## Open Space

In the places we studied, open space is typically some combination of hardscaped plazas, green parks, and pocket parks, with treelined streets and trail networks leading to larger regional play areas and outlying reserves. The distinguishing factor in most of the best examples was the amount of, and degree of, emphasis on smaller, more diverse open spaces that interconnect, as opposed to a singular grand space. The average amount of land allocated to open space is generally between 5 and 15 percent.

# SQUARES, GREENS, AND PARKS

Large, urban outdoor spaces are indispensable to the public lives of our communities. We have observed that the best spaces magnify the city's energy and activity but also provide rest and relaxation in an urban context. Beyond this, we wanted to know what physical characteristics specifically make these great urban spaces so special. It was not difficult to formulate a list of high-quality urban spaces from around the country; their number and variety is considerable.

Our selection includes many of the most well known and historic examples of urban outdoor space, such as Boston Public Garden and Rockefeller Center; other examples, such as Santana Row and Belmar Town Center, are more recent creations that are generating considerable interest among planners, designers, and architects.

Our study combines a variety of diagrams that help us better understand the scale, layout, and workings of these spaces, including figure-ground diagrams of the site and surroundings, diagrammatic analyses of the site-plan arrangement, and sectional drawings depicting spatial enclosures. The information used to prepare these diagrams was drawn from a variety of sources, including aerial imagery, site visits, photos, and Web research.

# PUBLIC SPACES SUCCESSFUL INTERPLAY OF URBAN OPEN-SPACE ELEMENTS

Each place type described below plays a role in creating open and public space in urban districts. Each one has a specific function and relationship to the other elements. They are listed below from smallest element to largest.

*Places* (or "pocket parks") and passages are the smallest of urban spaces. They occur midblock or at contiguous corners where pedestrian movement patterns require a linkage between two major streets or activity areas.

*Shopping streets* must be carefully situated in order to best serve communities and complement surrounding urban spaces. Unlike squares and pocket parks, shopping streets are best located at the perimeter of a community, along home-bound routes that join up with a major boulevard. In these locations they can serve twice the catchment (communities on both sides of the boulevard will shop there), as opposed to being "buried" within a community without primary frontage. (Both places and shopping streets are studied in depth in later chapters.)

*Squares* are larger urban spaces and help to define an entire urban community if they are a major center of public events and activity. Squares are most successful when they combine amenities such as seating, public artwork, and a central activity space with informative signs, maps, restrooms, and security. Squares are best located at primary intersections in the center of an urban district or between two or more districts.

*Greens* are grassy open spaces that may be used passively or actively; they accommodate both unstructured play and programmed events. Traditionally, greens have been gathering spaces for town meetings and other large public events.

*Parks* are often the largest public spaces in a city and are regional destinations that accommodate a wide variety of recreational activities and major civic events. As such, their connection to an arterial street that serves the region is important to their success. Parks that share parking with surrounding commercial areas also help establish viable pedestrian movement patterns through the city.

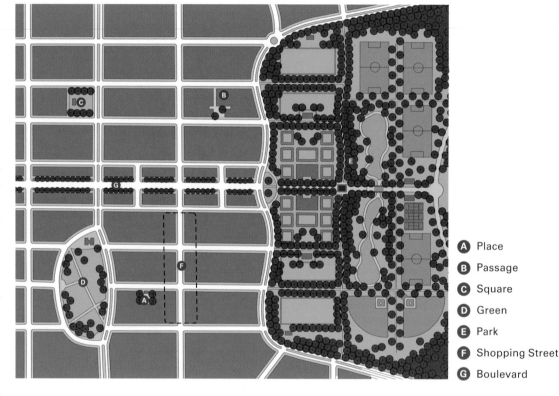

- **A** Place
- **B** Passage
- **C** Square
- **D** Green
- **E** Park
- **F** Shopping Street
- **G** Boulevard

# SQUARES ESSENTIAL CHARACTERISTICS

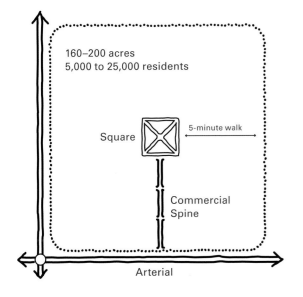

160–200 acres
5,000 to 25,000 residents

Square

5-minute walk

Commercial
Spine

Arterial

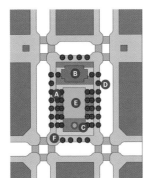

- **A** Canopy Shade Trees / Seating
- **B** Retail / Information Kiosk
- **C** Fountain / Public Art
- **D** On-Street Parking
- **E** Event Space
- **F** Curb Bulbs

Typical Enclosure (Section)

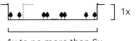

1x

1x to no more than 6x

Typical Proportions (Plan)

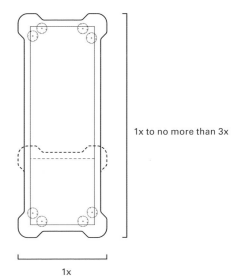

1x to no more than 3x

1x

Squares typically serve as activity centers for urban neighborhoods with 5,000 to 25,000 inhabitants, and they vary in size from one to roughly six acres. Residents ought to be able to walk to an urban square that is within five minutes or a quarter-mile radius of their home. The classic square is edged with wide sidewalks underneath canopy shade trees or trelliswork. Well-lit, informal seating areas often ring a central event space. Small kiosks or pavilions providing food, security, or information are common in squares. A landmark, such as a public art piece or fountain, provides a place for people to meet; fountains can also mitigate traffic noise. Needless changes in level often threaten the success of urban squares because they create pedestrian barriers and should be avoided. Parking is often handled best by parallel or angled on-street parking that lines the square's perimeter. At intersections, bulbouts reduce the distance pedestrians need to walk in order to cross the street;

they also calm traffic. Within squares, underground parking access should be designed carefully to avoid visual barriers that obstruct views into the space. The square's dimensions are important: its length should be no more than three times its width, and the ratio of enclosure needs to be carefully considered as well (see below).

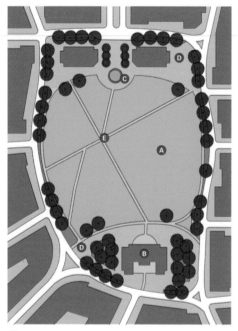

**A** Flexible Open Space / Primary Gathering Space

**B** Civic Area

**C** Primary Entry

**D** Secondary Function Area

**E** Diagonal Pathways

Depending on their size, greens can support roughly four times as many people as an urban square—typically somewhere between 20,000 and 100,000 residents. In agrarian communities, greens were used as flexible open space suitable for gatherings, recreation space, and communal grazing land. Churches, city halls, and other civic buildings were often incorporated within or adjacent to the green. Today, greens often weave recreational and cultural amenities into the city fabric; they complement, rather than compete with, the day-to-day functions of urban squares. Due to their size, greens typically have primary and secondary points of entry and a hierarchy of spaces composed of a central, open gathering area and smaller spaces surrounding it. Pathways through the green should be important pedestrian connections through the city.

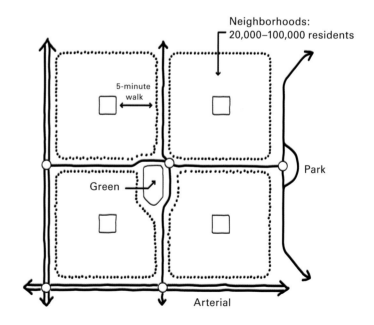

# PARKS ESSENTIAL CHARACTERISTICS

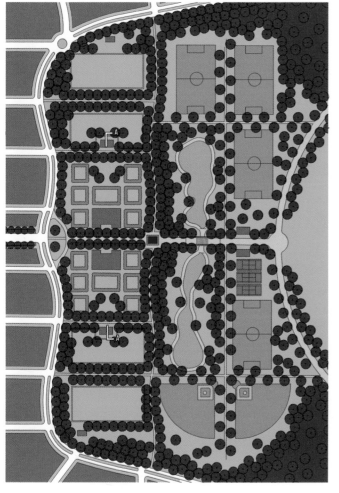

Parks are the largest type of public urban space and as such can address needs of communities outside of the urban core. They range in size from 10 acres to several thousand acres. Parks have amenities that smaller open spaces do not: natural features such as meadows, lakes, rivers, trails, and topography; recreational infrastructure such as sports-field complexes, ice rinks, and play equipment; and civic institutions such as museums, libraries, botanical gardens, zoos, and major event areas. Their edges provide a transitional area between the urban grid pattern and the parkland's interior. Gardens and small areas for passive recreation are typically located between pedestrian pathways that create a "procession," or a primary spine of pedestrian connection, through the park. This procession leads to various activity zones of individual character. Another important part of the park is the "objective"—the primary central gathering space at its heart. A part of the objective should be a large, open, grassy, and relatively flat area between two and 10 acres in size, where major concerts, public gatherings, and other events take place. It should also be a place where residents go to relax during lunchtime or on the weekends.

**A** City Grid

**B** Park Boundary

**C** Procession (Primary Axis)

**D** Parterres

**E** Objective

**F** Natural Feature

**G** Activity Areas

**H** Central Gathering Area

**I** Civic Institutions

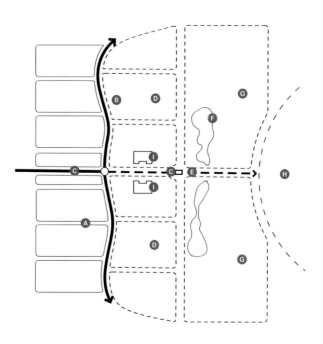

Central Axis

Active Space (Playfield)

Cultural Building

Passive Space (Garden)

Parterre    Axis    Parterre

bellevue downtown park
olympic sculpture park

jamison square
pioneer courthouse square

post office square
public garden

rockefeller center
union square
times square
bryant park

campus martius

millennium park

yerba buena gardens
union square
santana row

belmar town center

maguire gardens
pershing square    victoria gardens

centennial olympic park

southlake town square (park +plaza)    legacy town center
addison circle park

# SPATIAL ENCLOSURE

Spatial enclosure is the ratio of the average height of the buildings adjacent to the park to the park's width. Our study suggests that outdoor spaces with greater ratios of enclosure are often best when used more intensively and flexibly, in terms of the numbers and types of activities and visitors they can accommodate. Buildings surrounding parks provide a sense of shelter and comfort, but urban spaces located in dense urban cores must be able to handle intensive use and a variety of passive and active recreational activities. Minimum effective enclosure appears to be about 1:6, while maximum effective enclosure is about 3:1.

## Example (Full Enclosure)

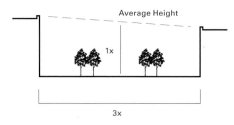

Resulting Ratio of Enclosure

## Example (Partial Enclosure)

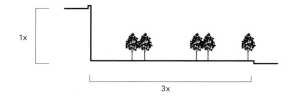

Resulting Ratio of Enclosure

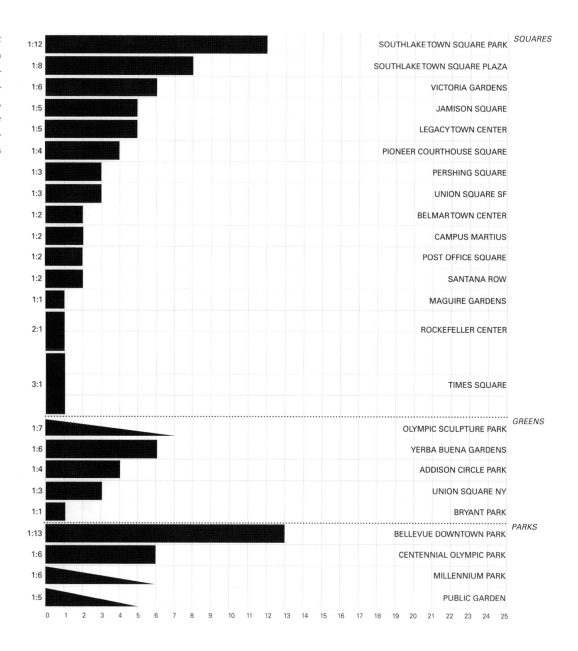

# PUBLIC SPACE SCALE COMPARISON

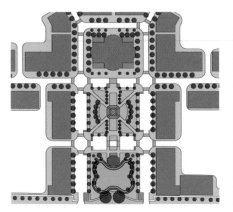

**SOUTHLAKE TOWN SQUARE**
(rustin park) Southlake, Texas
2.5 acres

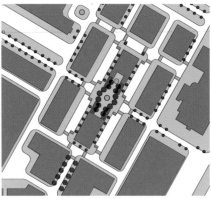

**SOUTHLAKE TOWN SQUARE**
(plaza at town square) Southlake, Texas
0.6 acres

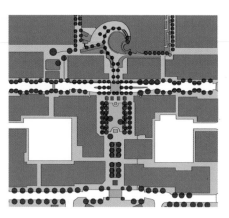

**VICTORIA GARDENS**
Rancho Cucamonga, California
2.25 acres

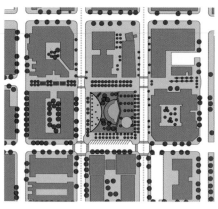

**JAMISON SQUARE**
Portland, Oregon
1.2 acres

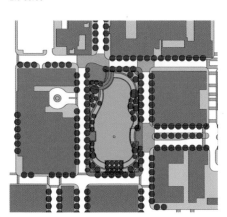

**LEGACY TOWN CENTER**
Plano, Texas
(bishop park) 1.2 acres

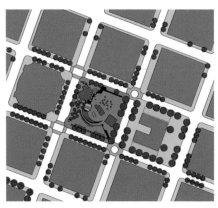

**PIONEER COURTHOUSE SQUARE**
Portland, Oregon
1.15 acres

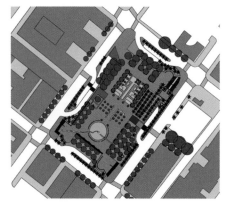

**PERSHING SQUARE**
Los Angeles
4.3 acres

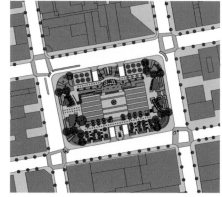

**UNION SQUARE**
San Francisco
3.5 acres

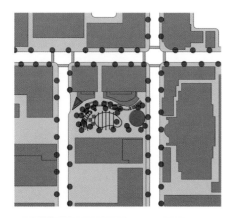

**BELMAR TOWN CENTER**
Lakewood, Colorado
1.2 acres

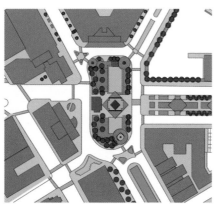

**CAMPUS MARTIUS**
Detroit
2.1 acres

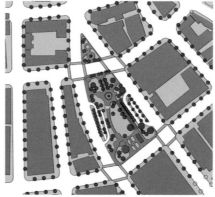

**POST OFFICE SQUARE**
Boston
1.7 acres

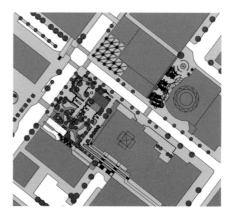

**MAGUIRE GARDENS**
Los Angeles
1.1 acres

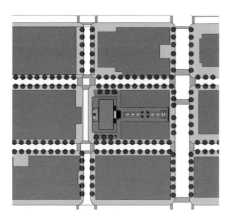

**ROCKEFELLER CENTER**
New York
1.0 acres

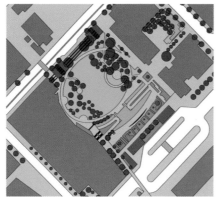

**YERBA BUENA GARDENS**
San Francisco
4.5 acres

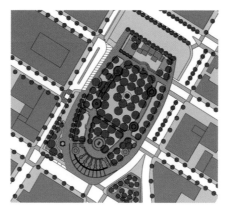

**UNION SQUARE**
New York
6.25 acres

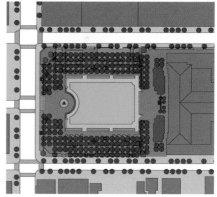

**BRYANT PARK**
New York
6.6 acres

# PUBLIC SPACE SCALE COMPARISON

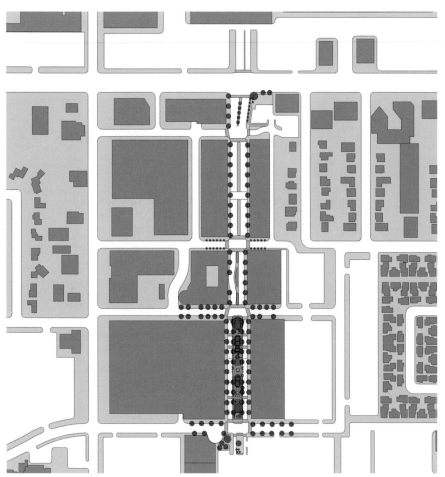

**SANTANA ROW**
San Jose, California
0.7 acres

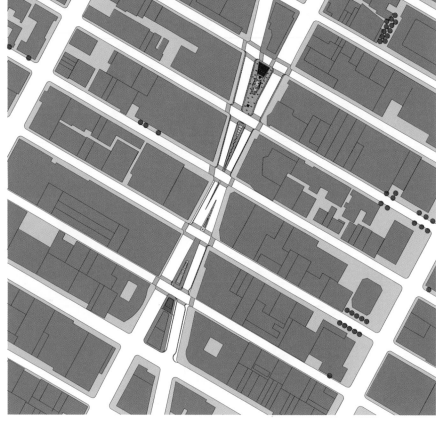

**TIMES SQUARE**
New York
0.75 acres

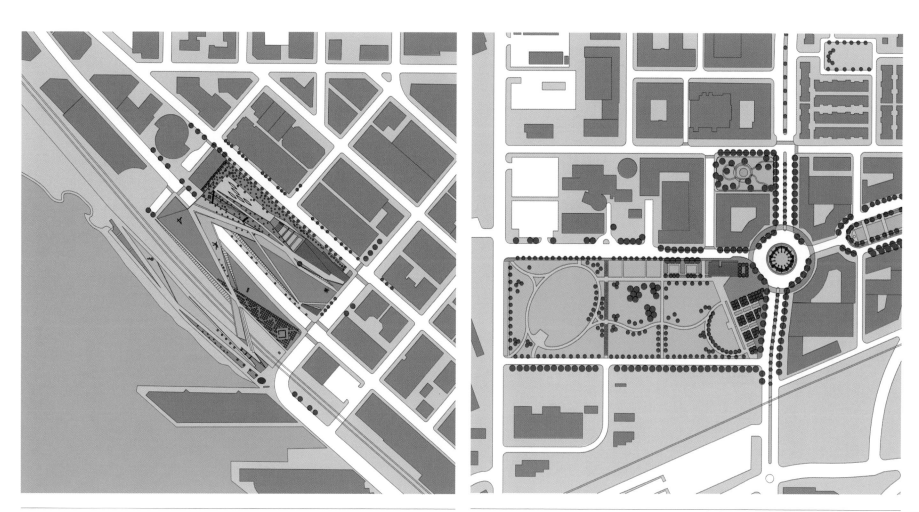

**OLYMPIC SCULPTURE PARK**
Seattle
9.0 acres

**ADDISON CIRCLE PARK**
Addison, Texas
11.0 acres

0'  200'
100'  400'

# PUBLIC SPACE SCALE COMPARISON

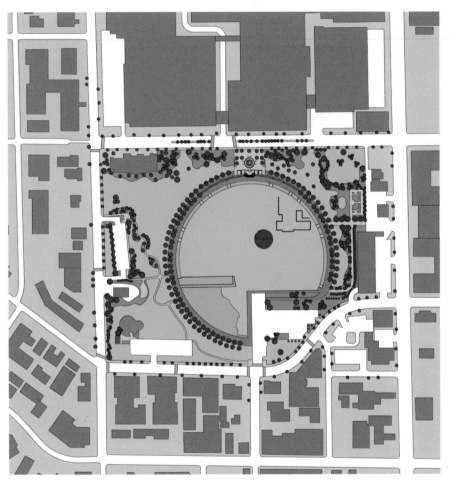

**BELLEVUE DOWNTOWN PARK**
Bellevue, Washington
21.2 acres

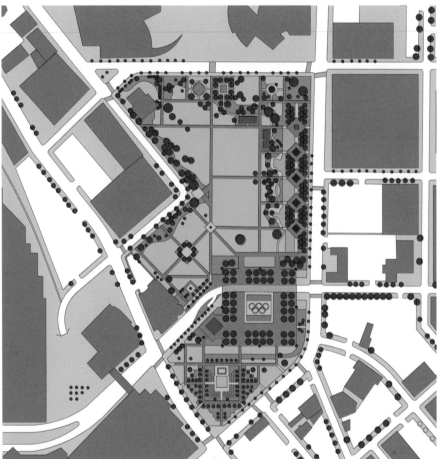

**CENTENNIAL OLYMPIC PARK**
Atlanta
21.0 acres

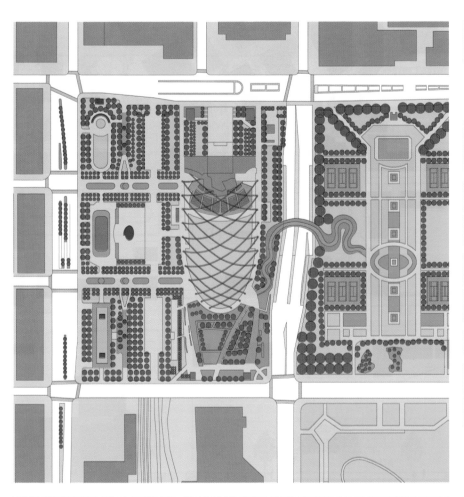

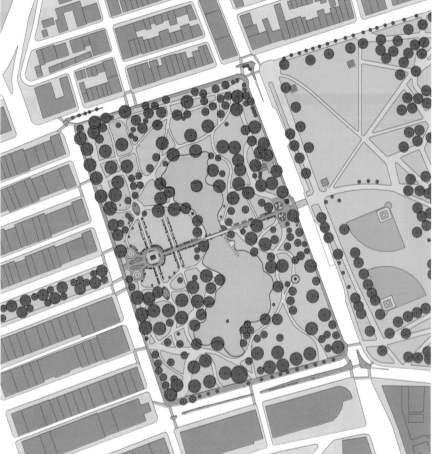

**MILLENNIUM PARK**
Chicago
23.0 acres

**BOSTON PUBLIC GARDEN**
Boston
23.1 acres

# VICTORIA GARDENS

Rancho Cucamonga, California

Victoria Gardens is a one-acre plaza sitting in the heart of a 60-acre retail and civic district in Rancho Cucamonga, California. Three department stores, a cinema, restaurants, and 150 specialty retailers occupy this regional shopping attraction. Lined with shops, Victoria Gardens has the feel of a traditional town green. Landscaping, retail kiosks, a water feature, and perimeter parking contribute to creating a pedestrian-friendly environment in the core. Events and programs take place throughout the year, both within the new civic auditorium and along the streets and plaza that are part of the project area. However, a lack of diversity of land use limits the ability of the district to function sustainably outside of typical shopping hours. Adding residential space, office space, or both within the core would help.

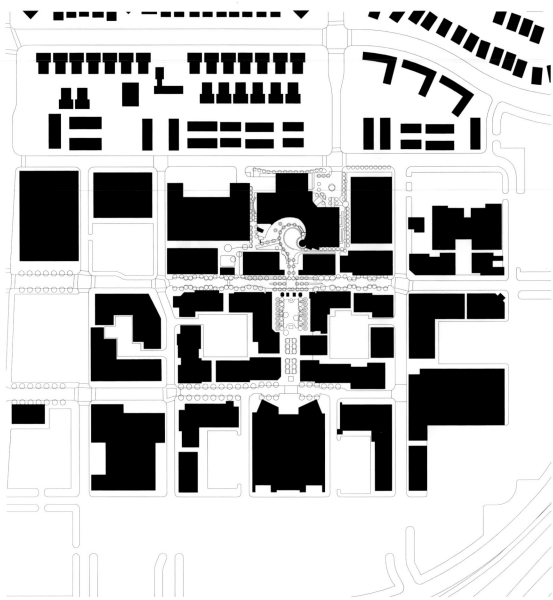

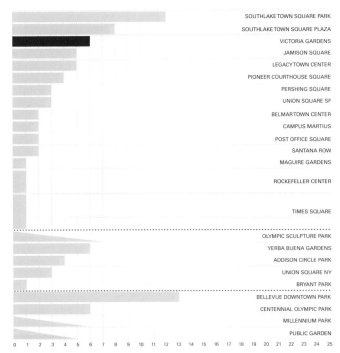

SOUTHLAKE TOWN SQUARE PARK
SOUTHLAKE TOWN SQUARE PLAZA
VICTORIA GARDENS
JAMISON SQUARE
LEGACY TOWN CENTER
PIONEER COURTHOUSE SQUARE
PERSHING SQUARE
UNION SQUARE SF
BELMAR TOWN CENTER
CAMPUS MARTIUS
POST OFFICE SQUARE
SANTANA ROW
MAGUIRE GARDENS

ROCKEFELLER CENTER

TIMES SQUARE

OLYMPIC SCULPTURE PARK
YERBA BUENA GARDENS
ADDISON CIRCLE PARK
UNION SQUARE NY
BRYANT PARK
BELLEVUE DOWNTOWN PARK
CENTENNIAL OLYMPIC PARK
MILLENNIUM PARK
PUBLIC GARDEN

0  1  2  3  4  5  6  7  8  9  10  11  12  13  14  15  16  17  18  19  20  21  22  23  24  25

Ratio of Enclosure: **1:6**

Figure Ground

0'  200'
100'  400'

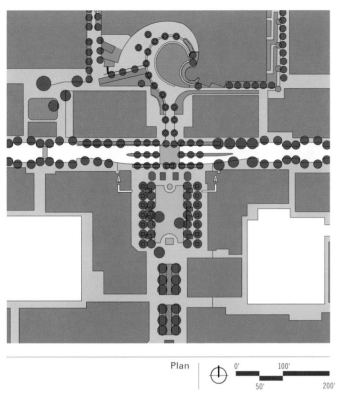

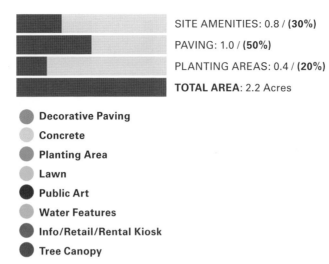

SITE AMENITIES: 0.8 / **(30%)**

PAVING: 1.0 / **(50%)**

PLANTING AREAS: 0.4 / **(20%)**

**TOTAL AREA**: 2.2 Acres

- Decorative Paving
- Concrete
- Planting Area
- Lawn
- Public Art
- Water Features
- Info/Retail/Rental Kiosk
- Tree Canopy

Plan

0'    50'    100'    200'

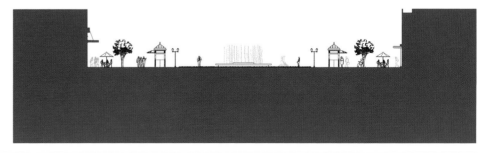

Section AA    0'    30'    60'

# Squares

# JAMISON SQUARE

Portland, Oregon

Jamison Square occupies a full city block in the Pearl District, a new arts-based redevelopment district adjacent to the downtown core. The square is a one-acre plot surrounded by high-density housing with ground-floor live/work units, cafés, retail spaces, and galleries. A fountain at the center of the square simulates a shallow tidal pool. There is café seating along the north side, where the street is closed to vehicular traffic. Passive seating areas and artwork ring the square, and walkways connect its corners to the center fountain. The square is the activity hub of the Pearl District and appropriately meets its needs as a gathering and meeting space.

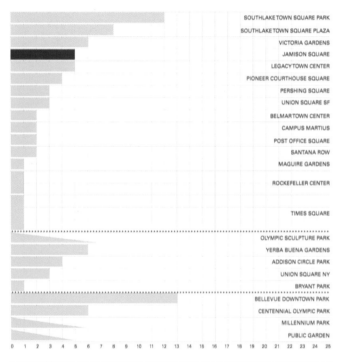

SOUTHLAKE TOWN SQUARE PARK
SOUTHLAKE TOWN SQUARE PLAZA
VICTORIA GARDENS
JAMISON SQUARE
LEGACY TOWN CENTER
PIONEER COURTHOUSE SQUARE
PERSHING SQUARE
UNION SQUARE SF
BELMAR TOWN CENTER
CAMPUS MARTIUS
POST OFFICE SQUARE
SANTANA ROW
MAGUIRE GARDENS
ROCKEFELLER CENTER
TIMES SQUARE
OLYMPIC SCULPTURE PARK
YERBA BUENA GARDENS
ADDISON CIRCLE PARK
UNION SQUARE NY
BRYANT PARK
BELLEVUE DOWNTOWN PARK
CENTENNIAL OLYMPIC PARK
MILLENNIUM PARK
PUBLIC GARDEN

Ratio of Enclosure: 1:5

Figure Ground

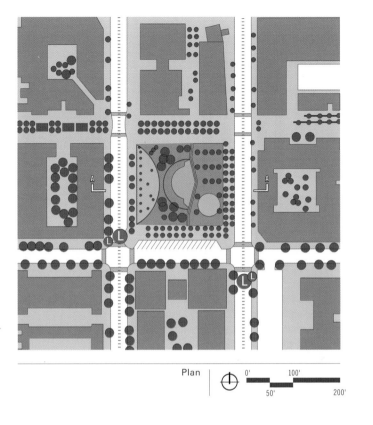

SITE AMENITIES: 0.1 / **(10%)**

PAVING: 0.8 / **(65%)**

PLANTING AREAS: 0.3 / **(25%)**

**TOTAL AREA:** 1.2 Acres

- Decorative Paving
- Concrete
- Planting Area
- Lawn
- Public Art
- Water Features
- Info/Retail/Rental Kiosk
- Tree Canopy

Ⓛ Light-Rail Stop

⋯⋯ Light-Rail Line

Plan    0'   100'
50'   200'

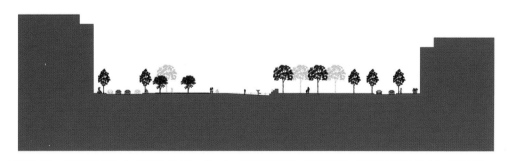

Section AA    0'   50'   100'

## Squares
# LEGACY TOWN CENTER
Plano, Texas

Legacy Town Center is at the heart of the 180-acre master planned community of Legacy in Plano, Texas. The town center contains a mix of residential, office, and hotel space. The project's core is Bishop Park, a three-acre space dominated by a large pond and complemented by plazas and walking paths. The park is the terminus of a boulevard that leads to the campus of Electronic Data Systems, the software firm that developed Legacy.

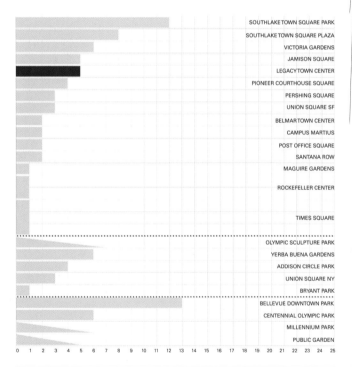

SOUTHLAKE TOWN SQUARE PARK
SOUTHLAKE TOWN SQUARE PLAZA
VICTORIA GARDENS
JAMISON SQUARE
LEGACY TOWN CENTER
PIONEER COURTHOUSE SQUARE
PERSHING SQUARE
UNION SQUARE SF
BELMAR TOWN CENTER
CAMPUS MARTIUS
POST OFFICE SQUARE
SANTANA ROW
MAGUIRE GARDENS

ROCKEFELLER CENTER

TIMES SQUARE

OLYMPIC SCULPTURE PARK
YERBA BUENA GARDENS
ADDISON CIRCLE PARK
UNION SQUARE NY
BRYANT PARK
BELLEVUE DOWNTOWN PARK
CENTENNIAL OLYMPIC PARK
MILLENNIUM PARK
PUBLIC GARDEN

0  1  2  3  4  5  6  7  8  9  10  11  12  13  14  15  16  17  18  19  20  21  22  23  24  25

Ratio of Enclosure: **1:5**

Figure Ground

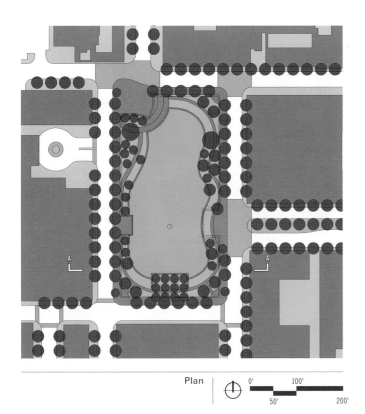

SITE AMENITIES: 1.6 / **(65%)**

PAVING: 0.1 / **(5%)**

PLANTING AREAS: 0.8 / **(30%)**

**TOTAL AREA:** 2.5 Acres

- Decorative Paving
- Concrete
- Planting Area
- Lawn
- Public Art
- Water Features
- Info/Retail/Rental Kiosk
- Tree Canopy

Plan

| 0'    100' |
| 50'    200' |

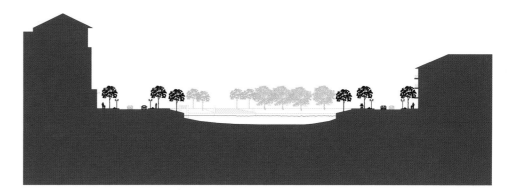

Section AA    | 0'    50'    100' |

# PIONEER COURTHOUSE SQUARE

Portland, Oregon

Located in downtown Portland, Oregon, Pioneer Courthouse Square is dubbed the city's "living room." With more than 26,000 people passing through the square each day, it is the most visited site in Portland. It hosts more than 300 events per year and features an outdoor theater, sculpture, seating areas, a waterfall, and an information kiosk. Public transit is readily available and used equally by residents, tourists, and workers who travel through the area. Downtown office and public buildings, hotels, and retailers all benefit from proximity to the square. Numerous level changes allow a variety of activities to occur simultaneously within a relatively compact space.

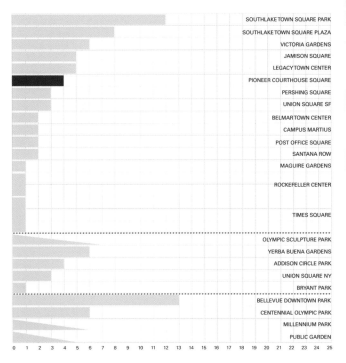

SOUTHLAKE TOWN SQUARE PARK
SOUTHLAKE TOWN SQUARE PLAZA
VICTORIA GARDENS
JAMISON SQUARE
LEGACY TOWN CENTER
PIONEER COURTHOUSE SQUARE
PERSHING SQUARE
UNION SQUARE SF
BELMAR TOWN CENTER
CAMPUS MARTIUS
POST OFFICE SQUARE
SANTANA ROW
MAGUIRE GARDENS

ROCKEFELLER CENTER

TIMES SQUARE

OLYMPIC SCULPTURE PARK
YERBA BUENA GARDENS
ADDISON CIRCLE PARK
UNION SQUARE NY
BRYANT PARK
BELLEVUE DOWNTOWN PARK
CENTENNIAL OLYMPIC PARK
MILLENNIUM PARK
PUBLIC GARDEN

0  1  2  3  4  5  6  7  8  9  10  11  12  13  14  15  16  17  18  19  20  21  22  23  24  25

Ratio of Enclosure: **1:4**

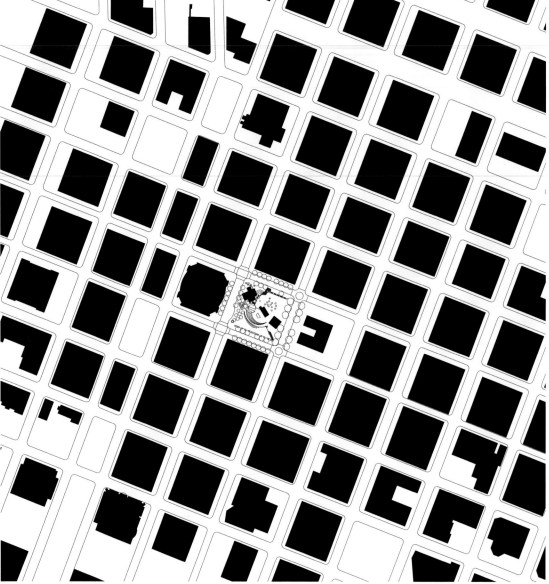

Figure Ground

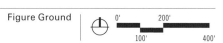

0'          200'
100'        400'

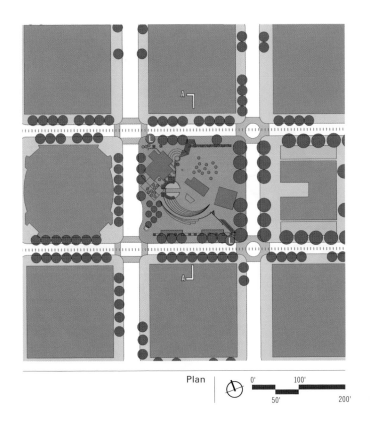

SITE AMENITIES: 0.3 / **(25%)**

PAVING: 0.9 / **(75%)**

PLANTING AREAS: 0.0 / **(0%)**

**TOTAL AREA**: 1.2 Acres

- Decorative Paving
- Concrete
- Planting Area
- Lawn
- Public Art
- Water Features
- Info/Retail/Rental Kiosk
- Tree Canopy

Ⓛ Light-Rail Stop

Plan | 0' 50' 100' 200'

Section AA | 0' 50' 100'

## Squares
# PERSHING SQUARE
Los Angeles

Pershing Square has been the primary public gathering space in downtown Los Angeles throughout the city's history. Redesigned in the mid-1990s, it is now an outdoor concert and event venue hosting free programs, above an underground garage that has 1,800 parking spaces. Parking ramps create significant pedestrian barriers to the park, restricting the accessibility and visibility of the square. The recent conversion of nearby buildings to mixed use and residential space has increased the level of activity in the square.

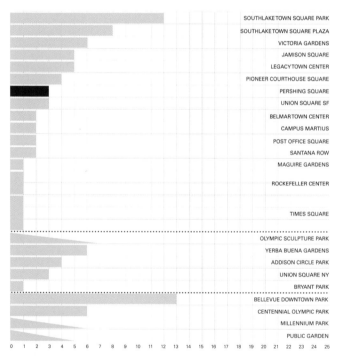

SOUTHLAKE TOWN SQUARE PARK
SOUTHLAKE TOWN SQUARE PLAZA
VICTORIA GARDENS
JAMISON SQUARE
LEGACY TOWN CENTER
PIONEER COURTHOUSE SQUARE
PERSHING SQUARE
UNION SQUARE SF
BELMAR TOWN CENTER
CAMPUS MARTIUS
POST OFFICE SQUARE
SANTANA ROW
MAGUIRE GARDENS

ROCKEFELLER CENTER

TIMES SQUARE

OLYMPIC SCULPTURE PARK
YERBA BUENA GARDENS
ADDISON CIRCLE PARK
UNION SQUARE NY
BRYANT PARK
BELLEVUE DOWNTOWN PARK
CENTENNIAL OLYMPIC PARK
MILLENNIUM PARK
PUBLIC GARDEN

0  1  2  3  4  5  6  7  8  9  10  11  12  13  14  15  16  17  18  19  20  21  22  23  24  25

Ratio of Enclosure: **1:3**

Figure Ground

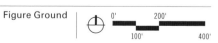

0'    200'
100'    400'

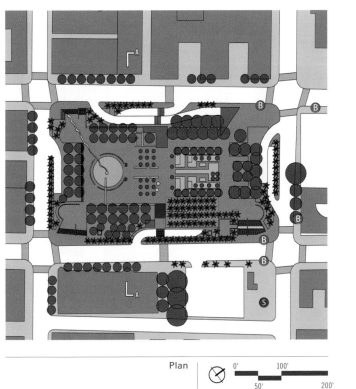

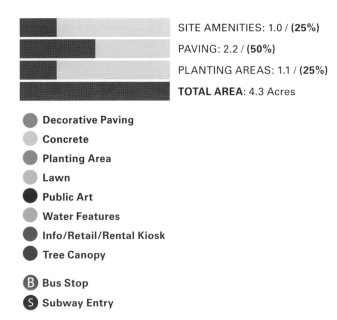

SITE AMENITIES: 1.0 / **(25%)**

PAVING: 2.2 / **(50%)**

PLANTING AREAS: 1.1 / **(25%)**

**TOTAL AREA**: 4.3 Acres

- Decorative Paving
- Concrete
- Planting Area
- Lawn
- Public Art
- Water Features
- Info/Retail/Rental Kiosk
- Tree Canopy

**B** Bus Stop

**S** Subway Entry

Plan   0'   50'   100'   200'

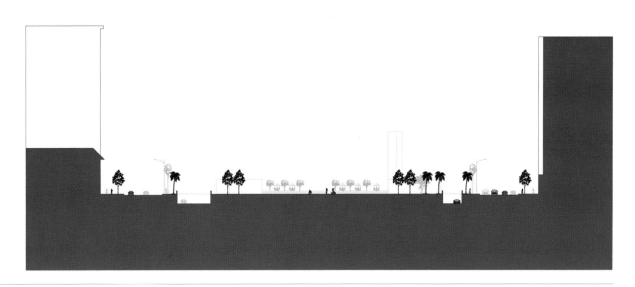

Section AA   0'   50'   100'

## Squares
# UNION SQUARE
San Francisco

Union Square, which contains 2.6 acres of open space in the downtown San Francisco, is the most significant shopping, hotel, and theater district in the city. The square and the areas surrounding it feature unique shops, department stores, boutiques, hotels, and theaters that attract large numbers of visitors. As a shopping destination, it contributes to the vitality of downtown San Francisco. The square is also a site for public concerts, protests, speeches, and holiday events, making it a dynamic and vital open space in downtown.

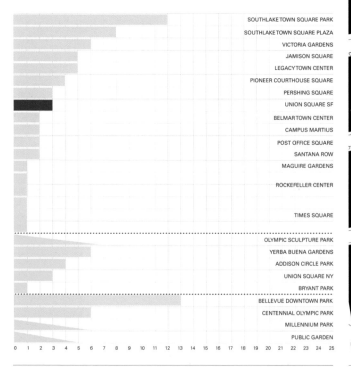

SOUTHLAKE TOWN SQUARE PARK
SOUTHLAKE TOWN SQUARE PLAZA
VICTORIA GARDENS
JAMISON SQUARE
LEGACY TOWN CENTER
PIONEER COURTHOUSE SQUARE
PERSHING SQUARE
UNION SQUARE SF
BELMAR TOWN CENTER
CAMPUS MARTIUS
POST OFFICE SQUARE
SANTANA ROW
MAGUIRE GARDENS

ROCKEFELLER CENTER

TIMES SQUARE

OLYMPIC SCULPTURE PARK
YERBA BUENA GARDENS
ADDISON CIRCLE PARK
UNION SQUARE NY
BRYANT PARK
BELLEVUE DOWNTOWN PARK
CENTENNIAL OLYMPIC PARK
MILLENNIUM PARK
PUBLIC GARDEN

0 1 2 3 4 5 6 7 8 9 10 11 12 13 14 15 16 17 18 19 20 21 22 23 24 25

Ratio of Enclosure: **1:3**

Figure Ground

0'   200'
100'   400'

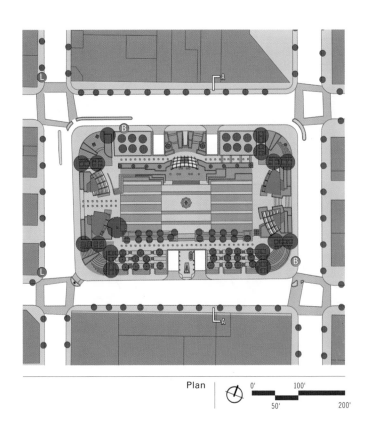

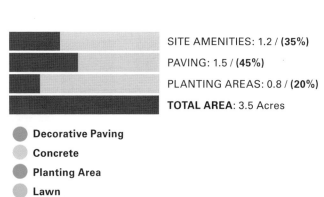

SITE AMENITIES: 1.2 / **(35%)**

PAVING: 1.5 / **(45%)**

PLANTING AREAS: 0.8 / **(20%)**

**TOTAL AREA**: 3.5 Acres

Decorative Paving

Concrete

Planting Area

Lawn

Public Art

Water Features

Info/Retail/Rental Kiosk

Tree Canopy

B Bus Stop

L Light-Rail Stop

⁙ Light-Rail Line

Plan | ⊕ | 0'   100'
50'   200'

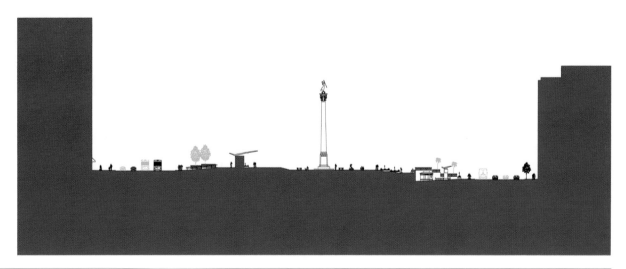

Section AA | 0'   50'   100'

# BELMAR TOWN CENTER

Lakewood, Colorado

Occupying the former site of a regional mall, Belmar was built to create a true mixed use downtown in Lakewood, Colorado. Belmar takes up 22 city blocks and contains stores, entertainment venues, residences, a museum, grocery stores, and office space. A central plaza with outdoor dining areas is the heart of the project. The plaza accommodates events throughout the year, including concerts, market days, and ice skating.

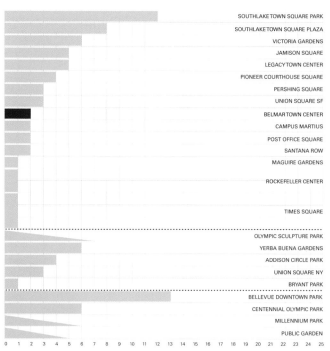

SOUTHLAKE TOWN SQUARE PARK
SOUTHLAKE TOWN SQUARE PLAZA
VICTORIA GARDENS
JAMISON SQUARE
LEGACY TOWN CENTER
PIONEER COURTHOUSE SQUARE
PERSHING SQUARE
UNION SQUARE SF
BELMAR TOWN CENTER
CAMPUS MARTIUS
POST OFFICE SQUARE
SANTANA ROW
MAGUIRE GARDENS

ROCKEFELLER CENTER

TIMES SQUARE

OLYMPIC SCULPTURE PARK
YERBA BUENA GARDENS
ADDISON CIRCLE PARK
UNION SQUARE NY
BRYANT PARK
BELLEVUE DOWNTOWN PARK
CENTENNIAL OLYMPIC PARK
MILLENNIUM PARK
PUBLIC GARDEN

0 1 2 3 4 5 6 7 8 9 10 11 12 13 14 15 16 17 18 19 20 21 22 23 24 25

Ratio of Enclosure: **1:2**

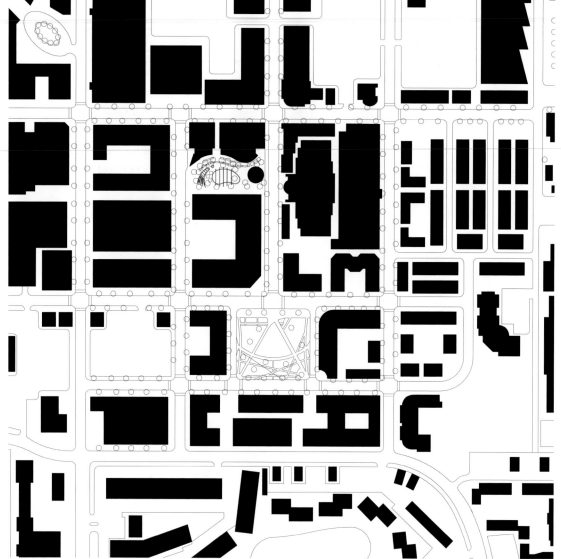

Figure Ground

0'     200'
100'     400'

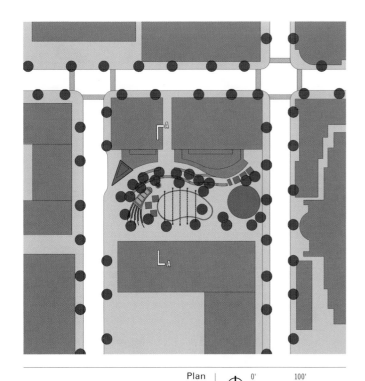

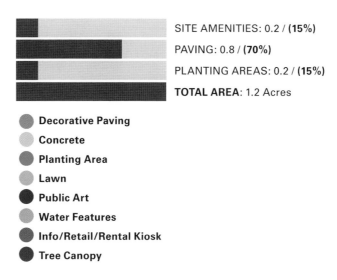

SITE AMENITIES: 0.2 / **(15%)**

PAVING: 0.8 / **(70%)**

PLANTING AREAS: 0.2 / **(15%)**

**TOTAL AREA**: 1.2 Acres

- Decorative Paving
- Concrete
- Planting Area
- Lawn
- Public Art
- Water Features
- Info/Retail/Rental Kiosk
- Tree Canopy

Plan | 0' 50' 100' 200'

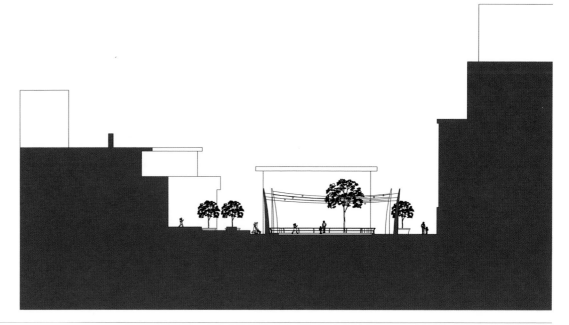

Section AA | 0' 25' 50'

# CAMPUS MARTIUS

Detroit

Once a parade ground, Campus Martius was redeveloped in the 1990s as a grand public space to anchor the heart of Detroit's urban core. Its strategic location at the confluence of six axial streets makes it a primary orientation point and gathering space for the entire downtown core. Ground-floor retail along its perimeter and aggressive events programming ensure that it is an attractive year-round destination. The central space is used as a concert venue in summer and an ice rink in the winter. Surrounding office space and convenience retail animate the space during weekday lunchtimes.

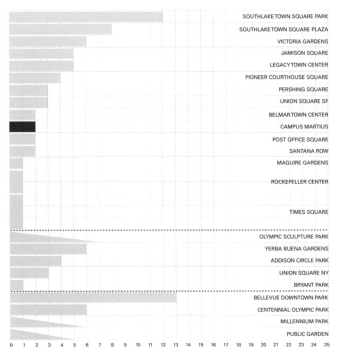

SOUTHLAKE TOWN SQUARE PARK
SOUTHLAKE TOWN SQUARE PLAZA
VICTORIA GARDENS
JAMISON SQUARE
LEGACY TOWN CENTER
PIONEER COURTHOUSE SQUARE
PERSHING SQUARE
UNION SQUARE SF
BELMAR TOWN CENTER
CAMPUS MARTIUS
POST OFFICE SQUARE
SANTANA ROW
MAGUIRE GARDENS
ROCKEFELLER CENTER
TIMES SQUARE
OLYMPIC SCULPTURE PARK
YERBA BUENA GARDENS
ADDISON CIRCLE PARK
UNION SQUARE NY
BRYANT PARK
BELLEVUE DOWNTOWN PARK
CENTENNIAL OLYMPIC PARK
MILLENNIUM PARK
PUBLIC GARDEN

0  1  2  3  4  5  6  7  8  9  10  11  12  13  14  15  16  17  18  19  20  21  22  23  24  25

Ratio of Enclosure: **1:2**

Figure Ground

0'          200'
100'          400'

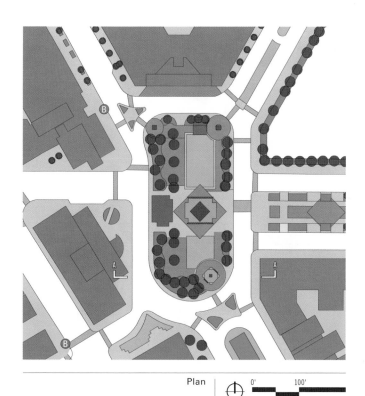

SITE AMENITIES: 0.3 / **(15%)**

PAVING: 1.2 / **(55%)**

PLANTING AREAS: 0.6 / **(20%)**

**TOTAL AREA**: 2.1 Acres

- Decorative Paving
- Concrete
- Planting Area
- Lawn
- Public Art
- Water Features
- Info/Retail/Rental Kiosk
- Tree Canopy

B Bus Stop

Plan | 0'    100'
     50'    200'

Section AA | 0'    50'    100'

## Squares
# POST OFFICE SQUARE
Boston

Once the site of an above-grade parking garage, Post Office Square was redeveloped in the 1980s as a multiuse park with below-grade parking. The square is used during the day by office workers and features a fountain, sculpture, and restaurant kiosks that are open throughout the year. Entries to the parking ramp are located along the length of the park and create pedestrian and visual barriers that hurt the effectiveness of the park as an amenity to adjacent uses.

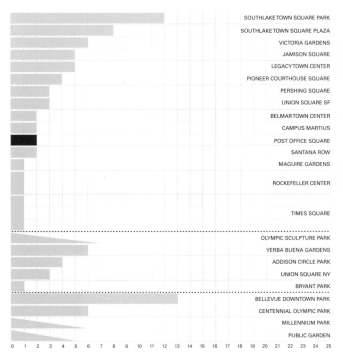

SOUTHLAKE TOWN SQUARE PARK
SOUTHLAKE TOWN SQUARE PLAZA
VICTORIA GARDENS
JAMISON SQUARE
LEGACY TOWN CENTER
PIONEER COURTHOUSE SQUARE
PERSHING SQUARE
UNION SQUARE SF
BELMAR TOWN CENTER
CAMPUS MARTIUS
POST OFFICE SQUARE
SANTANA ROW
MAGUIRE GARDENS

ROCKEFELLER CENTER

TIMES SQUARE

OLYMPIC SCULPTURE PARK
YERBA BUENA GARDENS
ADDISON CIRCLE PARK
UNION SQUARE NY
BRYANT PARK
BELLEVUE DOWNTOWN PARK
CENTENNIAL OLYMPIC PARK
MILLENNIUM PARK
PUBLIC GARDEN

0 1 2 3 4 5 6 7 8 9 10 11 12 13 14 15 16 17 18 19 20 21 22 23 24 25

Ratio of Enclosure: **1:2**

Figure Ground

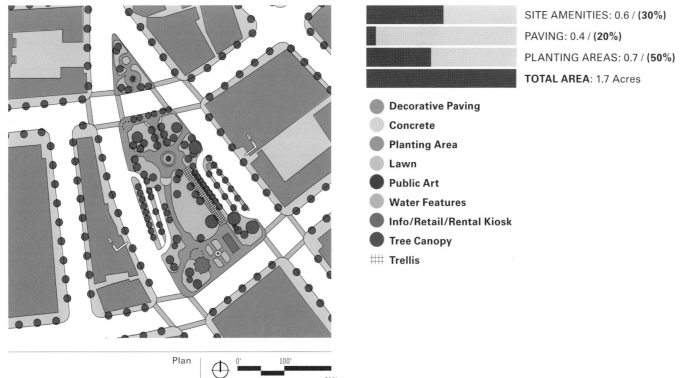

SITE AMENITIES: 0.6 / **(30%)**

PAVING: 0.4 / **(20%)**

PLANTING AREAS: 0.7 / **(50%)**

**TOTAL AREA**: 1.7 Acres

- Decorative Paving
- Concrete
- Planting Area
- Lawn
- Public Art
- Water Features
- Info/Retail/Rental Kiosk
- Tree Canopy
- ### Trellis

Plan    0'   100'    50'    200'

Section AA    0'   50'    100'

# Squares
# SANTANA ROW
San Jose, California

Santana Row gathers restaurants, retail, offices, and a hotel around a central shopping street. The boulevard accommodates two-way traffic; part of it expands around a large median. This median acts more like a "ramblas," activated with hardscaped, programmable event space and retail. The median contains relocated palm trees saved from the initial clearing of the site. An old church façade forms part of a retail kiosk in the median. Valley Fair Mall sits just north of the site and acts as a complementary shopping anchor.

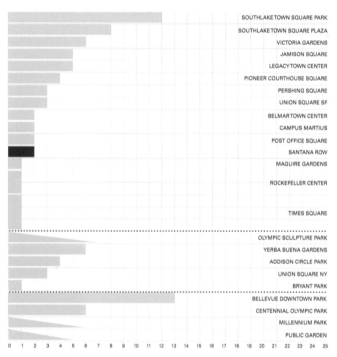

SOUTHLAKE TOWN SQUARE PARK
SOUTHLAKE TOWN SQUARE PLAZA
VICTORIA GARDENS
JAMISON SQUARE
LEGACY TOWN CENTER
PIONEER COURTHOUSE SQUARE
PERSHING SQUARE
UNION SQUARE SF
BELMAR TOWN CENTER
CAMPUS MARTIUS
POST OFFICE SQUARE
SANTANA ROW
MAGUIRE GARDENS
ROCKEFELLER CENTER
TIMES SQUARE
OLYMPIC SCULPTURE PARK
YERBA BUENA GARDENS
ADDISON CIRCLE PARK
UNION SQUARE NY
BRYANT PARK
BELLEVUE DOWNTOWN PARK
CENTENNIAL OLYMPIC PARK
MILLENNIUM PARK
PUBLIC GARDEN

0 1 2 3 4 5 6 7 8 9 10 11 12 13 14 15 16 17 18 19 20 21 22 23 24 25

Ratio of Enclosure: 1:2

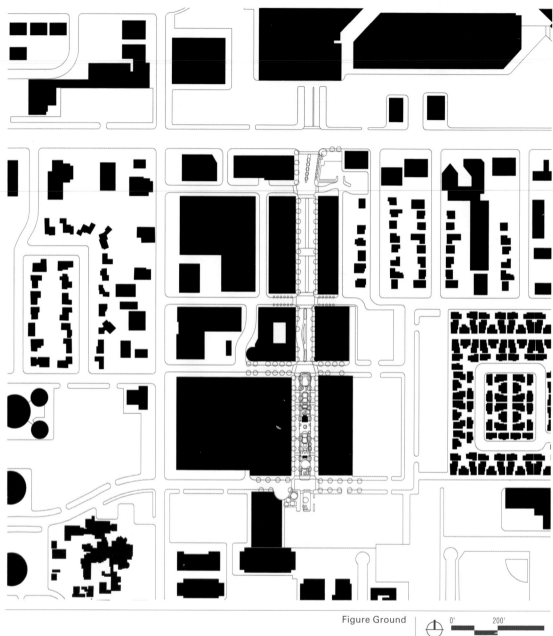

Figure Ground

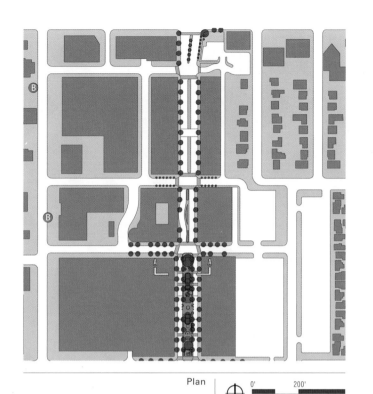

SITE AMENITIES: 0.2 / **(30%)**

PAVING: 0.2 / **(30%)**

PLANTING AREAS: 0.3 / **(40%)**

**TOTAL AREA**: 0.7 Acres

- ● Decorative Paving
- ○ Concrete
- ● Planting Area
- ○ Lawn
- ● Public Art
- ○ Water Features
- ● Info/Retail/Rental Kiosk
- ● Tree Canopy

- Ⓑ Bus Stop

Plan

0'   200'
100'   400'

Section AA        0'        10'        20'

# MAGUIRE GARDENS

Los Angeles

Maguire Gardens opened in 1991 on the site of a former parking lot next to the downtown branch of the Los Angeles Public Library. The park was developed on top of an underground parking structure serving the library and nearby office towers. Here the parking entry is handled in an effectively unobtrusive manner, adjacent to the main space. A number of notable art pieces are located in the garden, including *Spine*, by sculptor Jud Fine, which forms a procession from Flower Street to the main entrance of the library. A restaurant with outdoor seating generates daytime activity and hosts private functions during the evening.

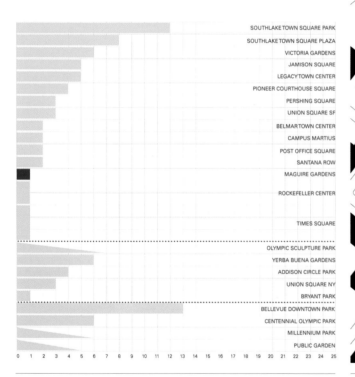

SOUTHLAKE TOWN SQUARE PARK
SOUTHLAKE TOWN SQUARE PLAZA
VICTORIA GARDENS
JAMISON SQUARE
LEGACY TOWN CENTER
PIONEER COURTHOUSE SQUARE
PERSHING SQUARE
UNION SQUARE SF
BELMAR TOWN CENTER
CAMPUS MARTIUS
POST OFFICE SQUARE
SANTANA ROW
MAGUIRE GARDENS
ROCKEFELLER CENTER
TIMES SQUARE
OLYMPIC SCULPTURE PARK
YERBA BUENA GARDENS
ADDISON CIRCLE PARK
UNION SQUARE NY
BRYANT PARK
BELLEVUE DOWNTOWN PARK
CENTENNIAL OLYMPIC PARK
MILLENNIUM PARK
PUBLIC GARDEN

0 1 2 3 4 5 6 7 8 9 10 11 12 13 14 15 16 17 18 19 20 21 22 23 24 25

Ratio of Enclosure: **1:1**

Figure Ground

0'    200'
100'    400'

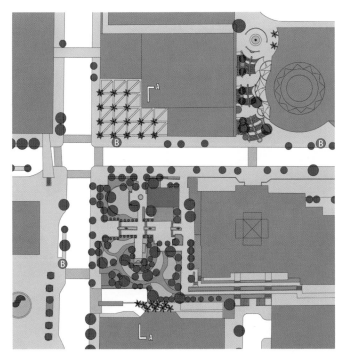

SITE AMENITIES: 0.15 / **(15%)**

PAVING: 0.4 / **(35%)**

PLANTING AREAS: 0.55 / **(50%)**

**TOTAL AREA**: 1.1 Acres

- Decorative Paving
- Concrete
- Planting Area
- Lawn
- Public Art
- Water Features
- Info/Retail/Rental Kiosk
- Tree Canopy

B Bus Stop

Plan     0'    100'
        50'    200'

Section AA     0'    50'    100'

# ROCKEFELLER CENTER

New York

Developed in the 1930s, Rockefeller Center is a complex of three outdoor spaces in the heart of Midtown Manhattan: the Fifth Avenue pedestrian entry, the Promenade Garden (and its elaborate fountain feature), and a sunken plaza space, which accommodates outdoor dining and events in the summer and skating in the winter. Midblock passages running through the site effectively break down the scale of the buildings and transform their assemblage into a human-scaled urban room.

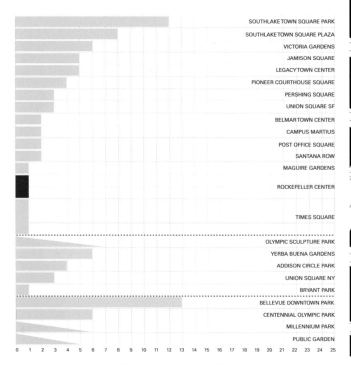

SOUTHLAKE TOWN SQUARE PARK
SOUTHLAKE TOWN SQUARE PLAZA
VICTORIA GARDENS
JAMISON SQUARE
LEGACY TOWN CENTER
PIONEER COURTHOUSE SQUARE
PERSHING SQUARE
UNION SQUARE SF
BELMAR TOWN CENTER
CAMPUS MARTIUS
POST OFFICE SQUARE
SANTANA ROW
MAGUIRE GARDENS

ROCKEFELLER CENTER

TIMES SQUARE

OLYMPIC SCULPTURE PARK
YERBA BUENA GARDENS
ADDISON CIRCLE PARK
UNION SQUARE NY
BRYANT PARK
BELLEVUE DOWNTOWN PARK
CENTENNIAL OLYMPIC PARK
MILLENNIUM PARK
PUBLIC GARDEN

0  1  2  3  4  5  6  7  8  9  10  11  12  13  14  15  16  17  18  19  20  21  22  23  24  25

Ratio of Enclosure: **2:1**

Figure Ground

0'          200'
100'          400'

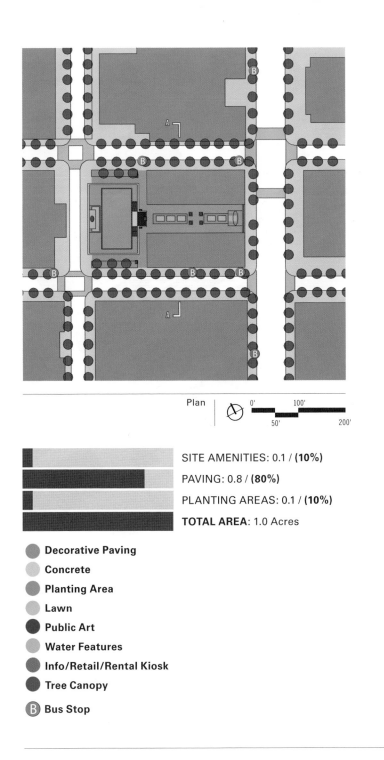

Plan

0'  50'  100'  200'

SITE AMENITIES: 0.1 / **(10%)**

PAVING: 0.8 / **(80%)**

PLANTING AREAS: 0.1 / **(10%)**

**TOTAL AREA**: 1.0 Acres

- Decorative Paving
- Concrete
- Planting Area
- Lawn
- Public Art
- Water Features
- Info/Retail/Rental Kiosk
- Tree Canopy
- B  Bus Stop

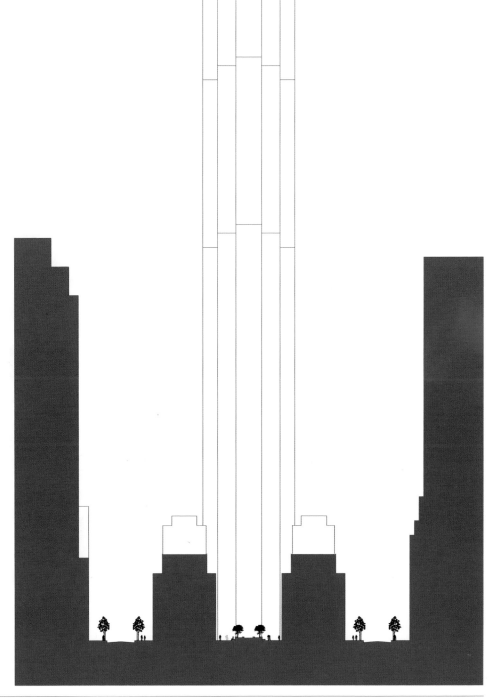

Section AA    0'   50'   100'

# TIMES SQUARE
New York

Times Square in Manhattan is formed by a major intersection at the junction of Broadway and Seventh Avenue. Surrounded by a large number of animated neon and digital advertisements (guidelines now require building owners to display signs of a minimum, not maximum, size), Times Square is a metonym for New York City itself. Its distinctive shops, restaurants, and live entertainment attract millions of visitors each year. City emphasis on redevelopment from the 1990s to today has resulted in the relocation of numerous media, entertainment, and financial companies to the area.

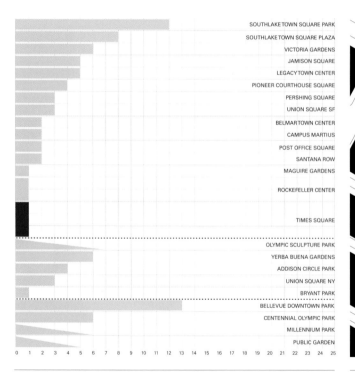

SOUTHLAKE TOWN SQUARE PARK
SOUTHLAKE TOWN SQUARE PLAZA
VICTORIA GARDENS
JAMISON SQUARE
LEGACY TOWN CENTER
PIONEER COURTHOUSE SQUARE
PERSHING SQUARE
UNION SQUARE SF
BELMAR TOWN CENTER
CAMPUS MARTIUS
POST OFFICE SQUARE
SANTANA ROW
MAGUIRE GARDENS

ROCKEFELLER CENTER

TIMES SQUARE

OLYMPIC SCULPTURE PARK
YERBA BUENA GARDENS
ADDISON CIRCLE PARK
UNION SQUARE NY
BRYANT PARK
BELLEVUE DOWNTOWN PARK
CENTENNIAL OLYMPIC PARK
MILLENNIUM PARK
PUBLIC GARDEN

0  1  2  3  4  5  6  7  8  9  10  11  12  13  14  15  16  17  18  19  20  21  22  23  24  25

Ratio of Enclosure: **3:1**

Figure Ground

0'    100'    200'    400'

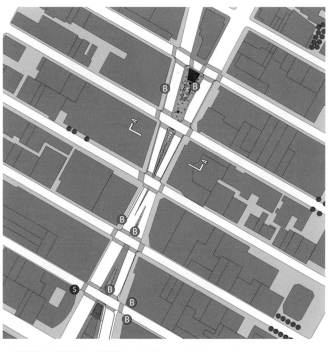

Plan

0'    100'    200'    400'

SITE AMENITIES: 0.2 / **(30%)**

PAVING: 0.6 / **(66%)**

PLANTING AREAS: 0.1 / **(4%)**

**TOTAL AREA**: 0.9 Acres

Decorative Paving

Concrete

Planting Area

Lawn

Public Art

Water Features

Info/Retail/Rental Kiosk

Tree Canopy

B  Bus Stop

S  Subway Entry

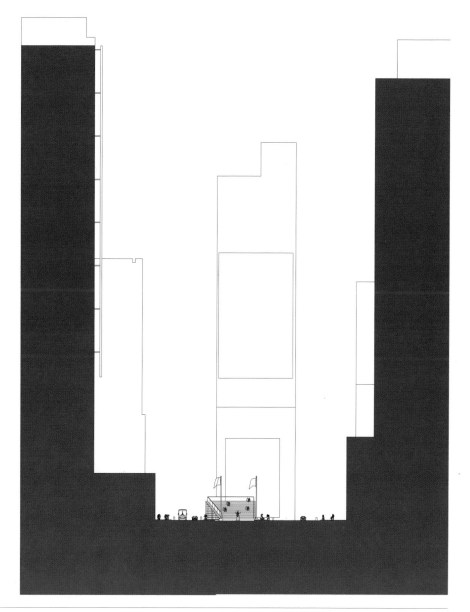

Section AA        0'    50'    100'

**Greens**
# OLYMPIC SCULPTURE PARK
Seattle

Located on the former site of petroleum transfer station, Olympic Sculpture Park, which opened in 2007, is the result of an international design competition sponsored by the Seattle Art Museum and the Trust for Public Land. The park features pathways and gardens that bridge a major roadway and active freight-rail lines and lead to the shore of Puget Sound, while mitigating the effects of more than 20 feet in level change. Public art in the park includes work by noted sculptors Richard Serra and Claes Oldenburg.

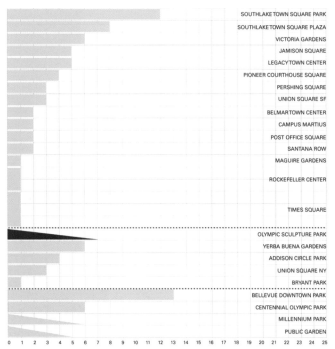

SOUTHLAKE TOWN SQUARE PARK
SOUTHLAKE TOWN SQUARE PLAZA
VICTORIA GARDENS
JAMISON SQUARE
LEGACY TOWN CENTER
PIONEER COURTHOUSE SQUARE
PERSHING SQUARE
UNION SQUARE SF
BELMAR TOWN CENTER
CAMPUS MARTIUS
POST OFFICE SQUARE
SANTANA ROW
MAGUIRE GARDENS
ROCKEFELLER CENTER
TIMES SQUARE
OLYMPIC SCULPTURE PARK
YERBA BUENA GARDENS
ADDISON CIRCLE PARK
UNION SQUARE NY
BRYANT PARK
BELLEVUE DOWNTOWN PARK
CENTENNIAL OLYMPIC PARK
MILLENNIUM PARK
PUBLIC GARDEN

0  1  2  3  4  5  6  7  8  9  10  11  12  13  14  15  16  17  18  19  20  21  22  23  24  25

Ratio of Enclosure: **1:7**

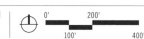

Figure Ground

0'          200'
100'          400'

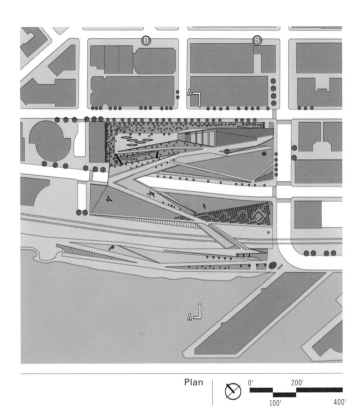

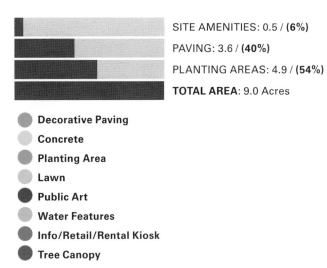

SITE AMENITIES: 0.5 / **(6%)**

PAVING: 3.6 / **(40%)**

PLANTING AREAS: 4.9 / **(54%)**

**TOTAL AREA**: 9.0 Acres

- Decorative Paving
- Concrete
- Planting Area
- Lawn
- Public Art
- Water Features
- Info/Retail/Rental Kiosk
- Tree Canopy
- Ⓑ Bus Stop

Plan   0'   200'
100'   400'

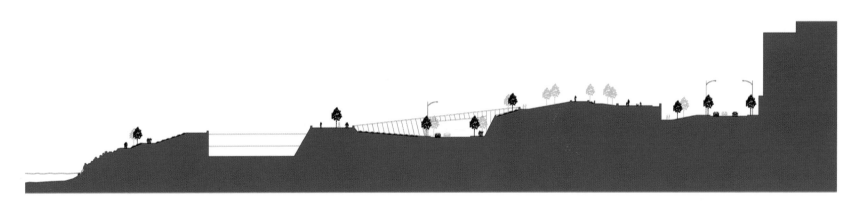

Section AA   0'   100'   200'

## Greens
# YERBA BUENA GARDENS
San Francisco

Yerba Buena was redeveloped as an arts and culture district in the 1990s. The threefold vision of the district was to bring art into the community, encourage diversity, and promote sustainability. The program includes three large museums, a cinema, a performing-arts space, a convention center, and an ice rink. The central green includes meadows, a water feature, public art pieces, small cafés, and event programs. The garden's transit linkages and proximity to Market Street make it an active hub for the entire city.

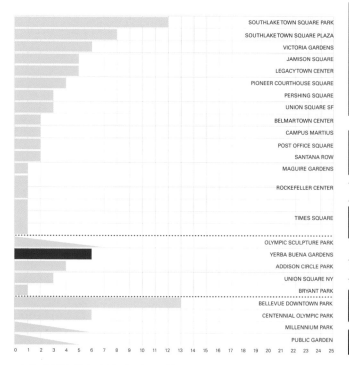

SOUTHLAKE TOWN SQUARE PARK
SOUTHLAKE TOWN SQUARE PLAZA
VICTORIA GARDENS
JAMISON SQUARE
LEGACY TOWN CENTER
PIONEER COURTHOUSE SQUARE
PERSHING SQUARE
UNION SQUARE SF
BELMAR TOWN CENTER
CAMPUS MARTIUS
POST OFFICE SQUARE
SANTANA ROW
MAGUIRE GARDENS

ROCKEFELLER CENTER

TIMES SQUARE

OLYMPIC SCULPTURE PARK
YERBA BUENA GARDENS
ADDISON CIRCLE PARK
UNION SQUARE NY
BRYANT PARK

BELLEVUE DOWNTOWN PARK
CENTENNIAL OLYMPIC PARK
MILLENNIUM PARK
PUBLIC GARDEN

0  1  2  3  4  5  6  7  8  9  10  11  12  13  14  15  16  17  18  19  20  21  22  23  24  25

Ratio of Enclosure: **1:6**

Figure Ground

0'    200'
100'    400'

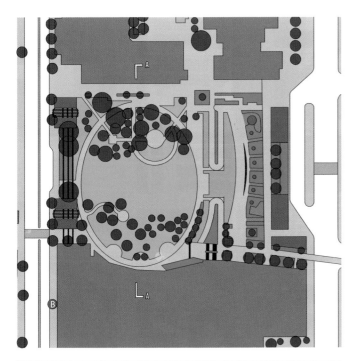

SITE AMENITIES: 1.2 / **(25%)**

PAVING: 1.5 / **(35%)**

PLANTING AREAS: 1.8 / **(40%)**

**TOTAL AREA**: 4.5 Acres

- Decorative Paving
- Concrete
- **Planting Area**
- Lawn
- Public Art
- Water Features
- Info/Retail/Rental Kiosk
- Tree Canopy
- (B) Bus Stop

Plan | 0' 100' / 50' 200'

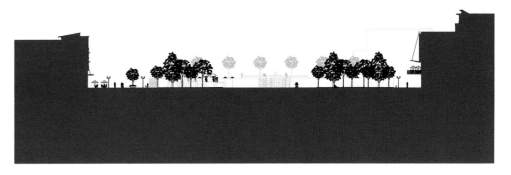

Section AA | 0' 50' 100'

**Greens**

# UNION SQUARE

New York

Redeveloped in the 1980s, Union Square is a popular meeting place because of its central location in Manhattan and its convergence of subway lines. There are bars and restaurants close to the square; some of them are among the city's most renowned. Lush landscaping, retail kiosks, a water feature, and perimeter parking all help make Union Square a successful public place. Events and programs take place throughout the year. The weekly farmers market is one of the largest in the city.

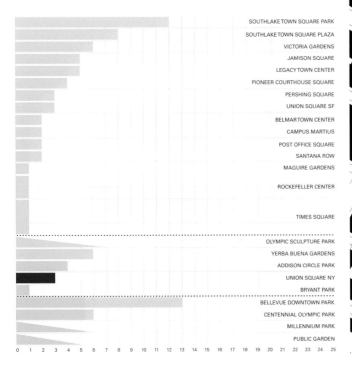

SOUTHLAKE TOWN SQUARE PARK
SOUTHLAKE TOWN SQUARE PLAZA
VICTORIA GARDENS
JAMISON SQUARE
LEGACY TOWN CENTER
PIONEER COURTHOUSE SQUARE
PERSHING SQUARE
UNION SQUARE SF
BELMAR TOWN CENTER
CAMPUS MARTIUS
POST OFFICE SQUARE
SANTANA ROW
MAGUIRE GARDENS

ROCKEFELLER CENTER

TIMES SQUARE

OLYMPIC SCULPTURE PARK
YERBA BUENA GARDENS
ADDISON CIRCLE PARK
UNION SQUARE NY
BRYANT PARK
BELLEVUE DOWNTOWN PARK
CENTENNIAL OLYMPIC PARK
MILLENNIUM PARK
PUBLIC GARDEN

0  1  2  3  4  5  6  7  8  9  10  11  12  13  14  15  16  17  18  19  20  21  22  23  24  25

Ratio of Enclosure: **1:3**

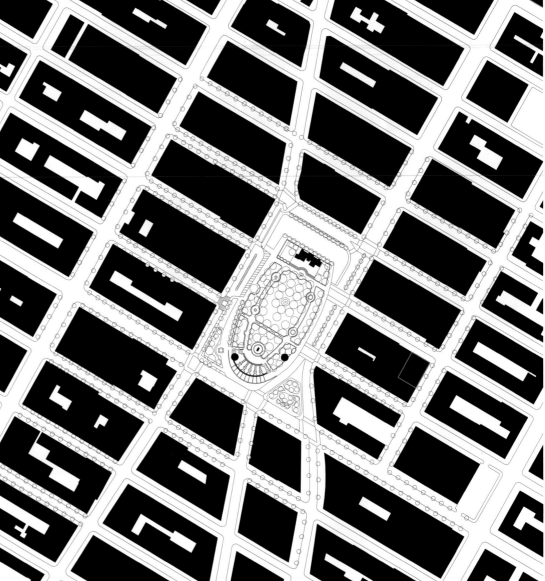

Figure Ground

0'          200'

100'          400'

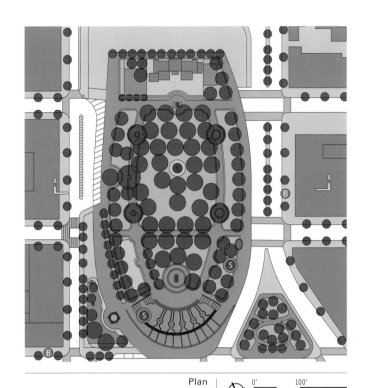

SITE AMENITIES: 1.0 / **(15%)**

PAVING: 3.0 / **(50%)**

PLANTING AREAS: 2.3 / **(35%)**

**TOTAL AREA**: 6.3 Acres

**Decorative Paving**

**Concrete**

**Planting Area**

**Lawn**

**Public Art**

**Water Features**

**Info/Retail/Rental Kiosk**

**Tree Canopy**

**B** **Bus Stop**

**S** **Subway Entry**

Plan    0'  100'  50'  200'

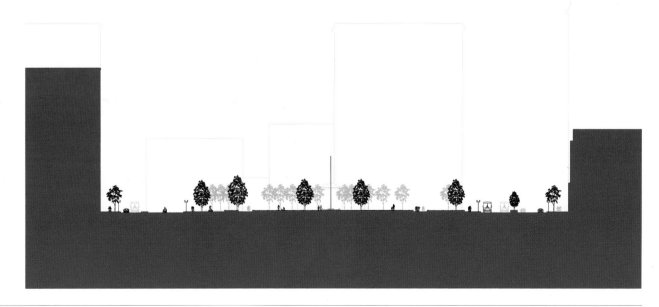

Section AA    0'  50'  100'

**Greens**
# BRYANT PARK
New York

In the center of Midtown Manhattan, Bryant Park contains a central green space surrounded by tree-lined seating areas, restaurants, food kiosks, and a large iconic fountain. Adjacent to the public library, whose stacks run underneath it, the park was renovated in the 1980s and now attracts more than 40,000 people each day. It provides a venue for various events throughout the year, such as the New York Film Festival and Fashion Week. Transit linkages are located around the site.

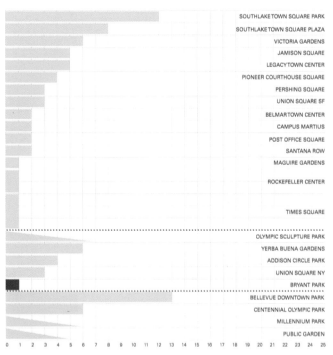

SOUTHLAKE TOWN SQUARE PARK
SOUTHLAKE TOWN SQUARE PLAZA
VICTORIA GARDENS
JAMISON SQUARE
LEGACY TOWN CENTER
PIONEER COURTHOUSE SQUARE
PERSHING SQUARE
UNION SQUARE SF
BELMAR TOWN CENTER
CAMPUS MARTIUS
POST OFFICE SQUARE
SANTANA ROW
MAGUIRE GARDENS
ROCKEFELLER CENTER
TIMES SQUARE
OLYMPIC SCULPTURE PARK
YERBA BUENA GARDENS
ADDISON CIRCLE PARK
UNION SQUARE NY
BRYANT PARK
BELLEVUE DOWNTOWN PARK
CENTENNIAL OLYMPIC PARK
MILLENNIUM PARK
PUBLIC GARDEN

0 1 2 3 4 5 6 7 8 9 10 11 12 13 14 15 16 17 18 19 20 21 22 23 24 25

Ratio of Enclosure: **1:1**

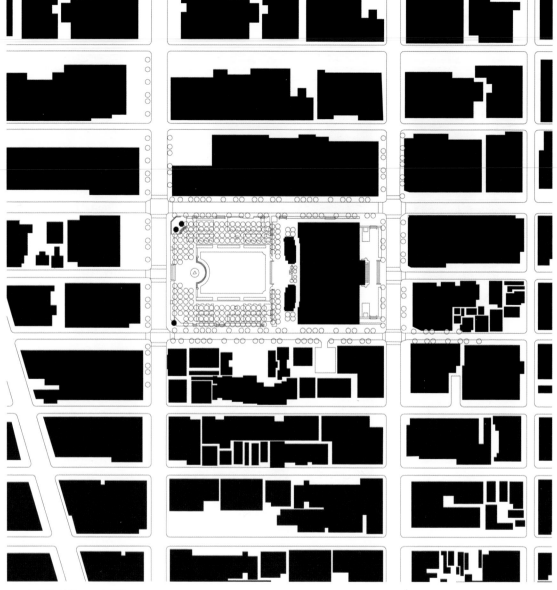

Figure Ground

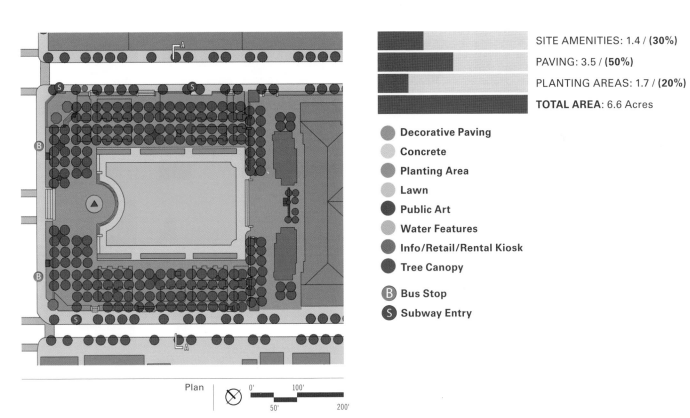

SITE AMENITIES: 1.4 / **(30%)**

PAVING: 3.5 / **(50%)**

PLANTING AREAS: 1.7 / **(20%)**

**TOTAL AREA**: 6.6 Acres

- Decorative Paving
- Concrete
- Planting Area
- Lawn
- Public Art
- Water Features
- Info/Retail/Rental Kiosk
- Tree Canopy

(B) Bus Stop

(S) Subway Entry

Plan

0'  100'
50'  200'

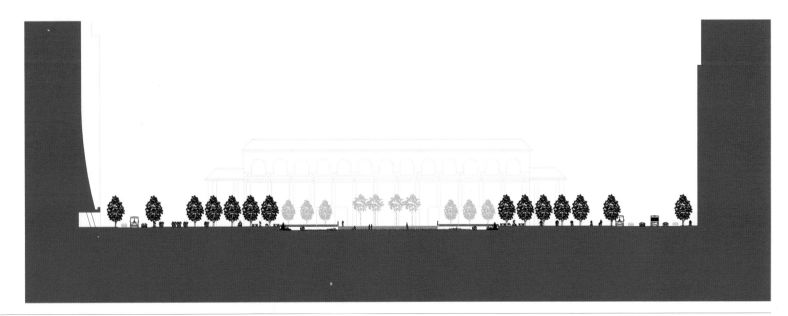

Section AA    0'    50'    100'

**Parks**

# BELLEVUE DOWNTOWN PARK

Bellevue, Washington

Developed between 1987 and 1990, Bellevue Downtown Park serves as the central event space for a Seattle suburb. The park's centerpiece is a lawn encircled by a tree-lined promenade. At the northern end of the park is a small plaza that accommodates a stage for large events. Other significant design elements include a large waterfall and reflecting pond, a rose garden, and benches near the remnant foundations of structures once part of the site.

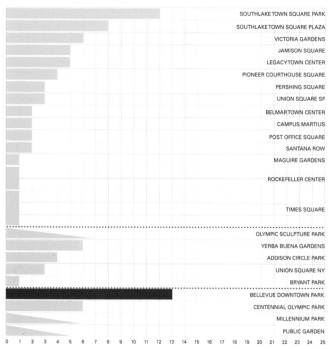

SOUTHLAKE TOWN SQUARE PARK
SOUTHLAKE TOWN SQUARE PLAZA
VICTORIA GARDENS
JAMISON SQUARE
LEGACY TOWN CENTER
PIONEER COURTHOUSE SQUARE
PERSHING SQUARE
UNION SQUARE SF
BELMAR TOWN CENTER
CAMPUS MARTIUS
POST OFFICE SQUARE
SANTANA ROW
MAGUIRE GARDENS
ROCKEFELLER CENTER

TIMES SQUARE

OLYMPIC SCULPTURE PARK
YERBA BUENA GARDENS
ADDISON CIRCLE PARK
UNION SQUARE NY
BRYANT PARK
BELLEVUE DOWNTOWN PARK
CENTENNIAL OLYMPIC PARK
MILLENNIUM PARK
PUBLIC GARDEN

0  1  2  3  4  5  6  7  8  9  10  11  12  13  14  15  16  17  18  19  20  21  22  23  24  25

Ratio of Enclosure: 1:13

Figure Ground

0'     200'
100'          400'

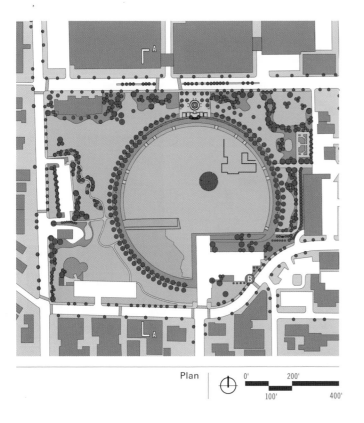

Plan | 0' 200' / 100' 400'

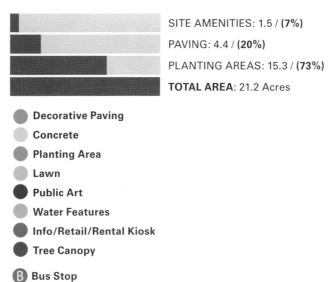

SITE AMENITIES: 1.5 / **(7%)**

PAVING: 4.4 / **(20%)**

PLANTING AREAS: 15.3 / **(73%)**

**TOTAL AREA**: 21.2 Acres

- Decorative Paving
- Concrete
- Planting Area
- Lawn
- Public Art
- Water Features
- Info/Retail/Rental Kiosk
- Tree Canopy

**B** Bus Stop

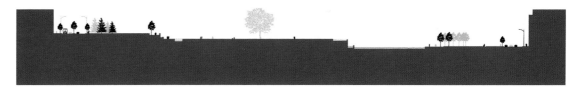

Section AA | 0' 100' 200'

**Parks**

# CENTENNIAL OLYMPIC PARK

Atlanta

Conceived as a hub for the 1996 Summer Olympic Games, Centennial Olympic Park was developed on 21 acres of surface parking. The park was modified after the games and has evolved into the primary outdoor event space in central Atlanta. The park serves as a link between the Georgia World Congress Center and the central business district. The park has spurred the development of nearby hotels, residences, and cultural institutions.

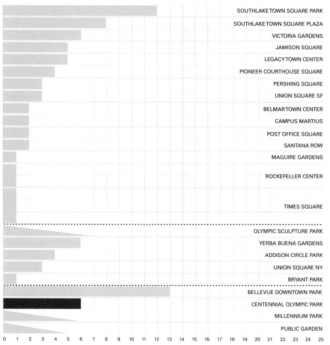

SOUTHLAKE TOWN SQUARE PARK
SOUTHLAKE TOWN SQUARE PLAZA
VICTORIA GARDENS
JAMISON SQUARE
LEGACY TOWN CENTER
PIONEER COURTHOUSE SQUARE
PERSHING SQUARE
UNION SQUARE SF
BELMAR TOWN CENTER
CAMPUS MARTIUS
POST OFFICE SQUARE
SANTANA ROW
MAGUIRE GARDENS

ROCKEFELLER CENTER

TIMES SQUARE

OLYMPIC SCULPTURE PARK
YERBA BUENA GARDENS
ADDISON CIRCLE PARK
UNION SQUARE NY
BRYANT PARK
BELLEVUE DOWNTOWN PARK
CENTENNIAL OLYMPIC PARK
MILLENNIUM PARK
PUBLIC GARDEN

0 1 2 3 4 5 6 7 8 9 10 11 12 13 14 15 16 17 18 19 20 21 22 23 24 25

Ratio of Enclosure: **1:6**

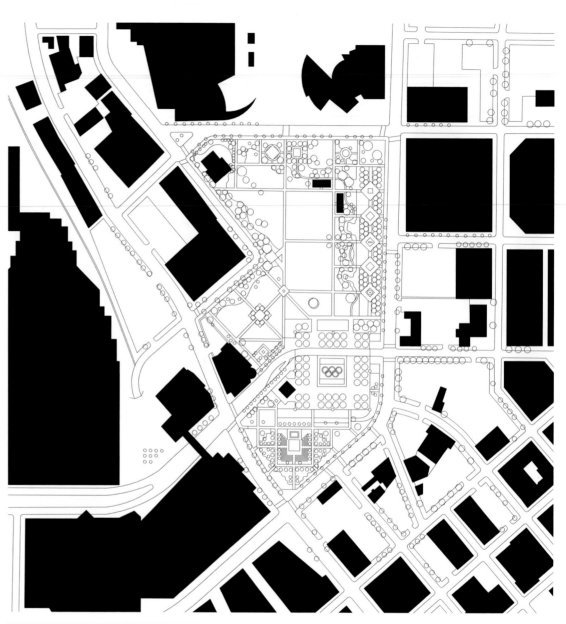

Figure Ground

0' 100' 200' 400'

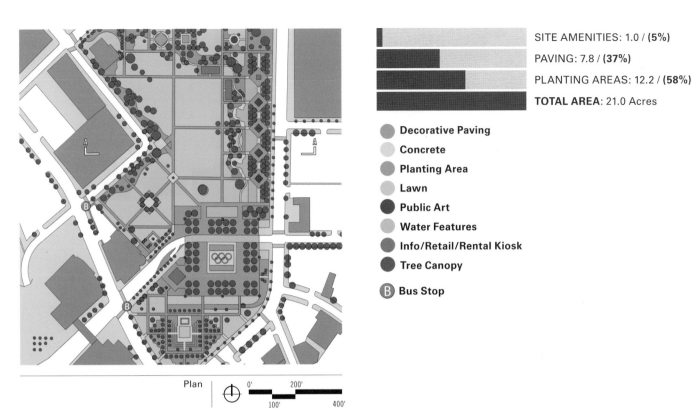

SITE AMENITIES: 1.0 / **(5%)**

PAVING: 7.8 / **(37%)**

PLANTING AREAS: 12.2 / **(58%)**

**TOTAL AREA**: 21.0 Acres

- Decorative Paving
- Concrete
- Planting Area
- Lawn
- Public Art
- Water Features
- Info/Retail/Rental Kiosk
- Tree Canopy

Ⓑ Bus Stop

Plan   0'   200'

100'   400'

Section AA   0'   50'   100'

# MILLENNIUM PARK

Chicago

Millennium Park is the result of a visionary mayor working in the early 1990s in collaboration with planners, architects, designers, and artists to build a park over an old railroad right-of-way. It has become a center for art, music, architecture, and landscape design in Chicago and has contributed to the renaissance of the Loop. Millennium Park features arguably the most interesting assemblage of outdoor spaces recently developed in the United States, including a concert venue, interactive fountain, and contemporary sculpture garden. Office buildings and residential lofts with views of the park now demand premium prices.

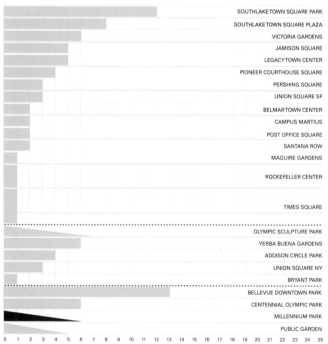

SOUTHLAKE TOWN SQUARE PARK
SOUTHLAKE TOWN SQUARE PLAZA
VICTORIA GARDENS
JAMISON SQUARE
LEGACY TOWN CENTER
PIONEER COURTHOUSE SQUARE
PERSHING SQUARE
UNION SQUARE SF
BELMAR TOWN CENTER
CAMPUS MARTIUS
POST OFFICE SQUARE
SANTANA ROW
MAGUIRE GARDENS
ROCKEFELLER CENTER
TIMES SQUARE
OLYMPIC SCULPTURE PARK
YERBA BUENA GARDENS
ADDISON CIRCLE PARK
UNION SQUARE NY
BRYANT PARK
BELLEVUE DOWNTOWN PARK
CENTENNIAL OLYMPIC PARK
MILLENNIUM PARK
PUBLIC GARDEN

0  1  2  3  4  5  6  7  8  9  10  11  12  13  14  15  16  17  18  19  20  21  22  23  24  25

Ratio of Enclosure: **1:2**

Figure Ground

0'    200'
100'    400'

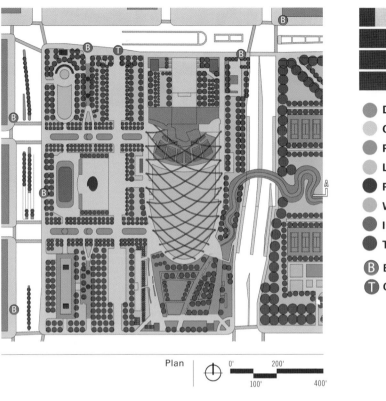

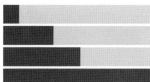

SITE AMENITIES: 3.0 / **(15%)**

PAVING: 8.0 / **(35%)**

PLANTING AREAS: 12.0 / **(50%)**

**TOTAL AREA**: 23.0 Acres

- Decorative Paving
- Concrete
- Planting Area
- Lawn
- Public Art
- Water Features
- Info/Retail/Rental Kiosk
- Tree Canopy
- **B** Bus Stop
- **T** Commuter Rail Station

Plan    0'   100'   200'   400'

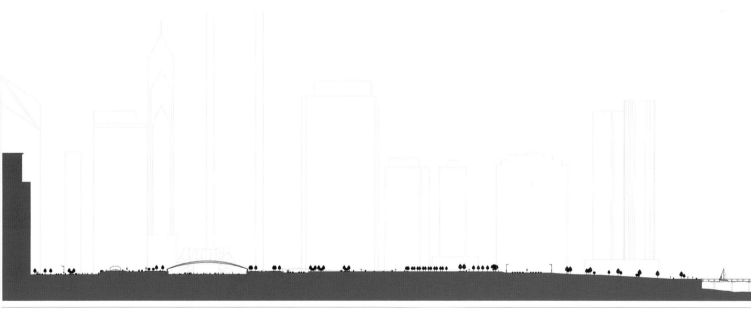

Section AA    0'   100'   200'   400'

**Parks**

# BOSTON PUBLIC GARDEN

Boston

The 24-acre park was established in 1837 as the first public botanical garden in the United States. The garden and nearby Boston Common form the northern terminus of Boston's Emerald Necklace—a long string of parks designed by Frederick Law Olmsted. Most of the common is an organic, relatively unstructured open space, while the Public Garden is more formal. It contains a lake in the center surrounded by formal plantings that change with the seasons. There are several commemorative statues as well as a small suspension bridge that articulates the space.

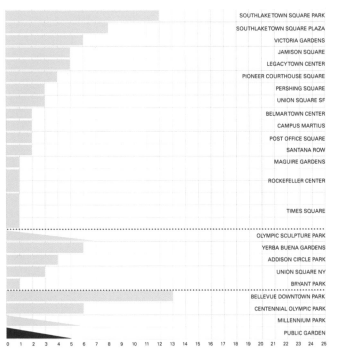

SOUTHLAKE TOWN SQUARE PARK
SOUTHLAKE TOWN SQUARE PLAZA
VICTORIA GARDENS
JAMISON SQUARE
LEGACY TOWN CENTER
PIONEER COURTHOUSE SQUARE
PERSHING SQUARE
UNION SQUARE SF
BELMAR TOWN CENTER
CAMPUS MARTIUS
POST OFFICE SQUARE
SANTANA ROW
MAGUIRE GARDENS
ROCKEFELLER CENTER
TIMES SQUARE
OLYMPIC SCULPTURE PARK
YERBA BUENA GARDENS
ADDISON CIRCLE PARK
UNION SQUARE NY
BRYANT PARK
BELLEVUE DOWNTOWN PARK
CENTENNIAL OLYMPIC PARK
MILLENNIUM PARK
PUBLIC GARDEN

0  1  2  3  4  5  6  7  8  9  10  11  12  13  14  15  16  17  18  19  20  21  22  23  24  25

Ratio of Enclosure: **1:10**

Figure Ground

0'    200'
100'    400'

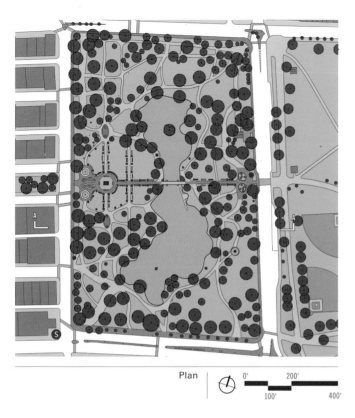

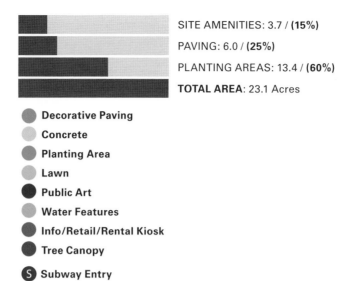

SITE AMENITIES: 3.7 / **(15%)**

PAVING: 6.0 / **(25%)**

PLANTING AREAS: 13.4 / **(60%)**

**TOTAL AREA**: 23.1 Acres

- Decorative Paving
- Concrete
- Planting Area
- Lawn
- Public Art
- Water Features
- Info/Retail/Rental Kiosk
- Tree Canopy
- **S** Subway Entry

Plan          0'      200'
             100'      400'

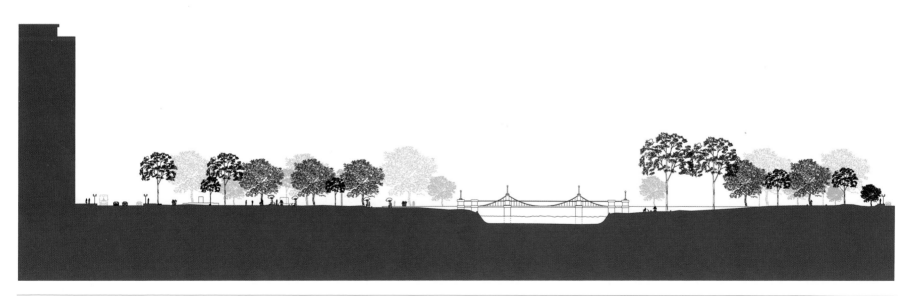

Section AA          0'      50'      100'

# SIZE OF OUTDOOR SPACES

All of the outdoor spaces we studied function as key public gathering areas, but their specific uses and attractions vary with their sizes and locations within their metropolitan regions. Smaller squares that measure approximately one to three acres are quite adaptable and serve a number of purposes within cities: they create an amenity for regional commercial centers (as in Legacy Town Center, Southlake Town Center, and Victoria Gardens); they offer a hub for neighborhood activities and smaller planned events (Addison Circle Park); and they draw attention to activity at the heart of the metropolitan core and attract visitors from far and wide (Campus Martius, Pioneer Courthouse Square, Rockefeller Center, and Times Square). Slightly larger squares and greens of approximately four to six acres are also a common feature at the center of major metropolitan areas; they have the advantage of accommodating a wide variety of daytime activities, as well as grander scheduled events, such as festivals that occur over a week or a season (Yerba Buena Gardens, Union Square [New York], and Bryant Park). The largest spaces—urban parks of 10 or more acres—attract a pool of downtown occupants, daytime workers, city and regional visitors who flock to parks as passive recreation or for planned events throughout the year (as in the case of Millennium Park and Boston Public Garden).

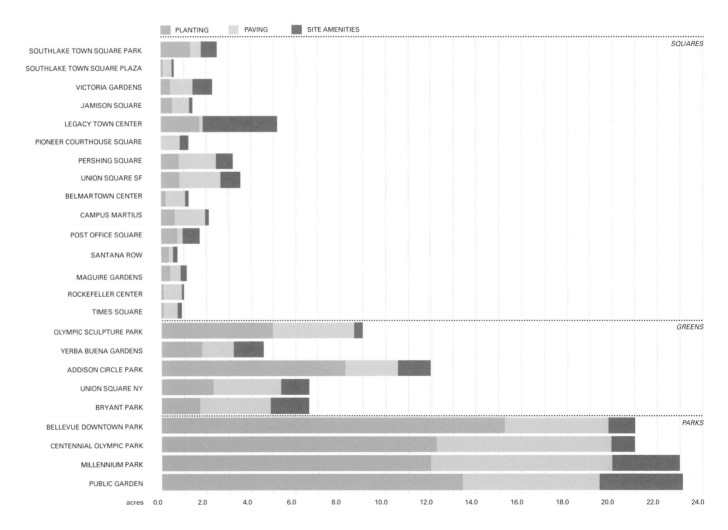

# PAVED AND PLANTED AREAS BY PERCENTAGE

Although squares should provide physical and psychological relief from the built environment, they often are surprisingly hardscaped in design with limited lawn or planted areas. In fact, our working definition of a square requires that more than 50 percent of the surface area is paved, which is a common characteristic among such spaces. Some of these squares are 80 to 90 percent hardscape, especially where intense use limits expansive planted areas (as is the case with Pioneer Courthouse Square and Times Square). Even the spaces we have classified as greens approach 50 percent hardscape in order to main-

tain suitable pedestrian access. This draws attention to the importance of using permeable paving and other sustainable materials. The sizes of lawns and plantings are less important than their design and placement. For example, suitably placed canopy trees help define outdoor "rooms" and provide shade; a central plot of grass often accommodates a variety of activities as well as paved areas, as long as foot traffic is limited on these areas during nonevent days.

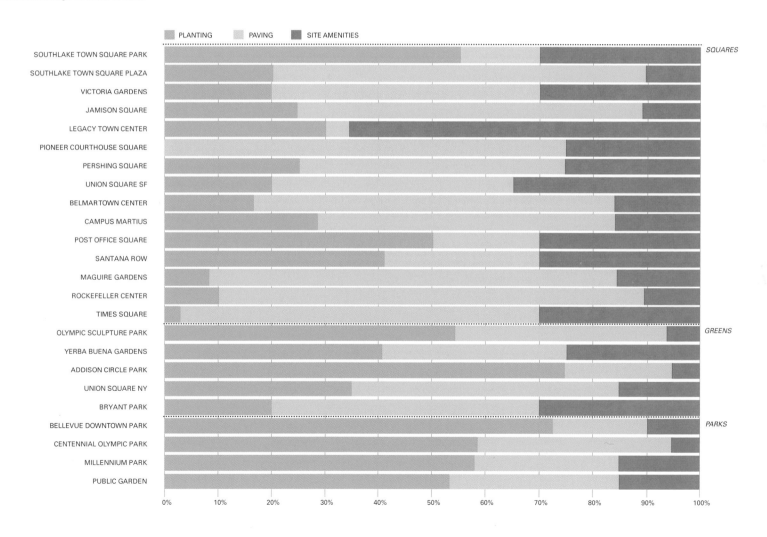

### Access

The most widely used, safest, and effective public open spaces are often accessible by citywide public-transit lines and major streets. They are located in high-density, mixed use areas where open space is needed the most.

### Plan Relationship

The shape of the space is important to its function. For example, squares or plazas with a width that is at least one third of its length often work best as gathering spaces. When width-to-length ratio exceeds 1:4, the space functions more like a median or esplanade that channels pedestrian movement.

### Spatial Enclosure

Most effective public spaces have a height-to-width ratio of at least 1:6. Spaces with less than that lack a sense of enclosure and as a result tend to lack a sense of place. Successful public spaces may have a spatial-enclosure ratio that is as high as 3:1.

### Scales of Activity

The most successful squares can accommodate a variety of activities simultaneously. Some squares are so well designed that a solitary person can read a book unbothered by a large, crowded event occurring simultaneously in another part of the square. This is most often achieved by setting aside the center as an unbroken event space and lining the perimeter with smaller "rooms" with canopy shade and seating areas.

### Event Space

At a minimum, event spaces should be a quarter acre in size; at a maximum, four acres. The most effective event space is unbroken lawn or pavement with paths around it. Events spaces are less effective when the pavement "cuts" the space into small pieces or when level changes break up the space unnecessarily. (Bryant Park has a good example of a flexible event space; Pershing Square is less successful because of level changes.)

### Focused Entries

Greens or squares work best when clustered design elements guide the viewer into the main space beyond. Views of the main space should never be significantly blocked in the entry sequence. Often "short side" intersection corners work best as primary pedestrian entries. Components of successful entries often include at-grade pedestrian access, a fountain feature, artwork, paved areas with fixed or movable seating, small retail kiosks, and perimeter shade

### Parterres

Parterres help separate different types of activity, organize paved and planted areas, and create movement patterns and linkages. In larger parks, the use of parterres provides a transition between the city grid and the larger open green areas within the park.

### Parking Impacts

Underground garages under greens or squares can accommodate the present and future parking needs of the district and free up nearby parcels for redevelopment. However, fitting parking under open space requires careful planning and design of the paved areas and careful selection of landscape features (such as specimen trees and planter beds) that place significant weight on the structure below. Ramps need to be strategically located to minimize the visual and physical barriers they present to pedestrians entering the area from surrounding streets.

# SHOPPING STREETS

In North American cities, many of the most interesting and active public spaces are shopping streets. They are found at the heart of our most vibrant mixed use districts and are fundamental to the renewal of our downtowns. How can we best understand and appreciate the special choreography of life on the shopping street? And how can we restore, re-create, cultivate, and propagate the experiences it provides?

In order to spend time walking, measuring, drawing, and studying shopping streets in some detail, we narrowed our focus to a few in and near Los Angeles. We identified five distinct types of shopping streets based on key physical characteristics and examined one example of each type to better understand what makes these places successful.

Our working definitions of the five types of shopping street are:

BOULEVARD: A tree-lined shopping street with multiple vehicular traffic lanes in each direction. Boulevards often have a planted median that accommodates pedestrian activity. Typically, boulevards have one lane of on-street parallel parking along each side.

MAIN STREET: A shopping street typically with a single car lane in each direction and no median. On-street angled or parallel parking along both sides of the street is common.

ARCADE: A shopping street with vehicular traffic lanes in each direction, flanked by arcades that cover all or most of the sidewalk. Arcades often have on-street angled or parallel parking along both sides of the street.

PROMENADE: A pedestrian-only shopping street fronted by buildings on each side. Vehicular cross traffic may be allowed between blocks.

BOARDWALK (or ESPLANADE): A shopping street fronted by buildings on one side. The open side often provides an expansive view of an open space beyond (such as a green space or body of water). Vehicular traffic is typically prohibited on a boardwalk.

Our study of each street includes an analysis of the surroundings, plan and section drawings based on aerial imagery, site reconnaissance, and field measurements. We include street dimensions and the design and placement of streetscape amenities, such as trees and outdoor furniture, wherever possible.

# SPATIAL ENCLOSURE / STREET DIMENSIONS AVERAGE DIMENSIONS OF SHOPPING STREETS

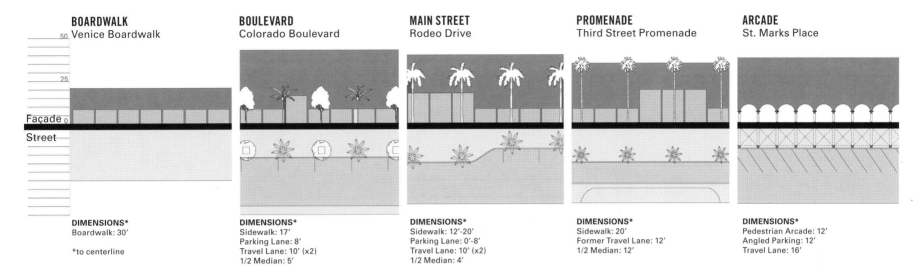

**BOARDWALK**
Venice Boardwalk

**BOULEVARD**
Colorado Boulevard

**MAIN STREET**
Rodeo Drive

**PROMENADE**
Third Street Promenade

**ARCADE**
St. Marks Place

Façade

Street

**DIMENSIONS***
Boardwalk: 30'

*to centerline

**DIMENSIONS***
Sidewalk: 17'
Parking Lane: 8'
Travel Lane: 10' (x2)
1/2 Median: 5'

**DIMENSIONS***
Sidewalk: 12'-20'
Parking Lane: 0'-8'
Travel Lane: 10' (x2)
1/2 Median: 4'

**DIMENSIONS***
Sidewalk: 20'
Former Travel Lane: 12'
1/2 Median: 12'

**DIMENSIONS***
Pedestrian Arcade: 12'
Angled Parking: 12'
Travel Lane: 16'

**Sidewalks:** Sidewalk width ranges from 12 to 25 feet, except on boardwalks, which are typically a bit wider than a sidewalk. For example, Venice Boardwalk is as wide as 30 feet in some places. A minimum sidewalk width of 12 feet is necessary for comfortable pedestrian flows; however, a somewhat wider dimension is recommended to accommodate streetscape amenities such as street trees and benches.

**Parking:** On-street parking is the norm where vehicular access is permitted. Parallel parking stalls are approximately eight to nine feet wide, adjacent to an 11- or 12-foot travel lane. Angled parking is also popular because it provides a greater number of total stalls and effectively slows traffic, due to the mechanics of backing out. Angled parking stalls are typically about 16 feet wide. Obviously, angled parking tends to widen the street section in comparison to parallel. Angled parking also tends to create a greater visual barrier between the street and the storefront.

**Travel Lanes:** Boulevards provide multiple lanes in each direction, while Main Streets provide a single lane in each direction; in both cases, the typical width of a travel lane should be 11 or 12 feet. Travel lanes that are significantly wider should be avoided because fast-moving traffic is inconsistent with the purpose of shopping streets, which should promote slow, steady traffic and pedestrian movement. The typical 16-foot travel lanes along angled-parking configurations are important to simultaneously accommodate cars backing out from angled parking stalls while maintaining reasonable vehicular speeds.

**Median:** Medians widen a typical street section and should be used carefully in the design of shopping streets. If the median is intended as an activity space, the width can be 50 feet or more (Mizner Park). However, they tend to be more effective if 30 feet or less (Santana Row). This is an important factor because one key aspect of an effective shopping experience is the interaction between one side of the street and the other. A 30-foot width allows for healthy plantings in the median while leaving enough space in the center for kiosks or event space. It is important not to use medians for traffic movements. Traffic

medians used as left-turn pockets tend not to be effective on shopping streets because they allow traffic to move too efficiently through the shopping environment, thereby compromising the experience for both pedestrians and drivers.

**Rhythm:** Good shopping streets establish a desirable rhythm among their tree plantings, arcade columns, and façade treatments that subscribe to human scale and amenity. Typical spacing between street trees is 25 to 30 feet, though spacings as wide as 50 feet and as narrow as 15 feet can be effective. Building modulations above storefronts should refer to a wider district or city scale. Building façades that visually refer to a dynamic between pedestrian and city scales are most effective along shopping streets.

**Enclosure:** Ratios of enclosure—the ratio of the average height of the buildings lining the street to the width of the street—are relatively consistent among the places we studied, measuring between 1:2 and 1:4. Higher ratios are common (1:1 is quite common along Michigan Avenue in Chicago, portions of Fifth Avenue in New York City can be 2:1), but lower ratios are not. A sense of enclosure is important for the life of the street because of its function as the heart of the district.

**Ratio of Enclosure:**

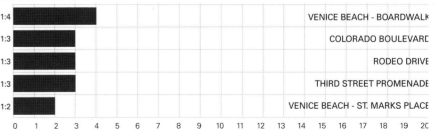

| | | |
|---|---|---|
| 1:4 | | VENICE BEACH - BOARDWALK |
| 1:3 | | COLORADO BOULEVARD |
| 1:3 | | RODEO DRIVE |
| 1:3 | | THIRD STREET PROMENADE |
| 1:2 | | VENICE BEACH - ST. MARKS PLACE |

0  1  2  3  4  5  6  7  8  9  10  11  12  13  14  15  16  17  18  19  20

# SHOPPING STREETS SCALE COMPARISON

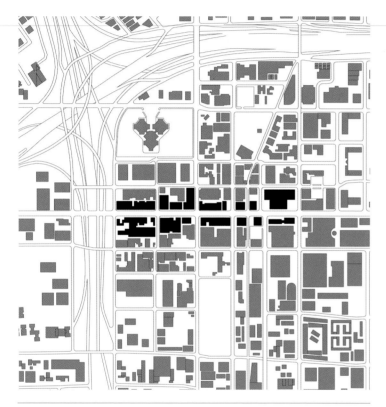

**COLORADO BOULEVARD**
Pasadena, California

**RODEO DRIVE**
Beverly Hills, California

**THIRD STREET PROMENADE**
Santa Monica, California

**VENICE BOARDWALK / ST. MARKS PLACE**
Venice, California

0'    600'
300'         1200'

# COLORADO BOULEVARD

Pasadena, California

As Pasadena's primary commercial corridor, Colorado Boulevard offers a variety of shops and restaurants in a historic downtown environment. Streetside dining and large storefront awnings encourage shoppers to walk. Upper stories include creative office and retail space. Historic Pasadena's downtown is served by two Metro Gold Line stations (Memorial Park Station and DelMar Station), as well as several bus routes that run along Colorado Boulevard. The city helped to finance the retrofitting of several historic buildings with elevators to facilitate adaptive reuse. There are parking structures at perimeter locations with pedestrian linkages to Colorado Boulevard.

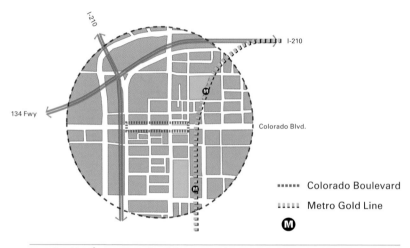

····· Colorado Boulevard

ııııı Metro Gold Line

Ⓜ

**Location Map | 1/4 mile radius** (1″ = 1/4 mile)

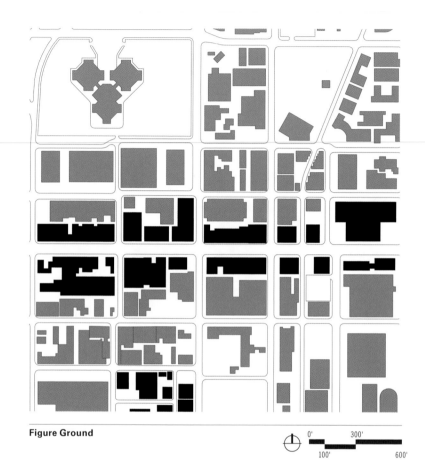

**Figure Ground**

0'        300'
100'        600'

■ Apparel: 64%

■ Restaurant: 25%

■ Home Furnishings: 7%

■ Cinema: 4%

**Land Use**

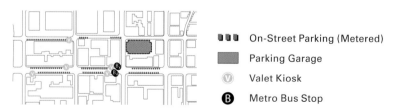

■■■ On-Street Parking (Metered)

■ Parking Garage

Ⓥ Valet Kiosk

Ⓑ Metro Bus Stop

**Parking and Servicing**

| STREET | DIMENSIONS | DESIGN |
| --- | --- | --- |
| building face-to-face | 99' ± | building setbacks vary between one and four feet |
| curb-to-curb | 64'-68' | curb line tapers at intersection approach to accommodate right-turn lane |
| travel lanes | 4 @ 10' each typical | two travel lanes in each direction |
| median | 10' typical | alternating left-turn pocket |
| parking lane | 8' typical | curbside, where permitted |
| sidewalk | 11'–17' | width varies depending on building setback |
| curb height | 5" | |

| TREES | SPACING | LOCATION | PLANTING CONDITION | DESIGN |
| --- | --- | --- | --- | --- |
| queen palm *(syagrus romanzoffiana)* | 45' on center, typical (16 per block) | 2'* on center, typical | decorative grate | tree types alternate |
| ginkgo *(ginkgo biloba)* | 45' on center, typical (16 per block) | 2'* on center, typical | decorative grate | tree types alternate |

| LIGHTING | SPACING | LOCATION |
| --- | --- | --- |
| overhead with traffic control | end-of-block (2 per block) | 1'* on center, typical |
| overhead with banner arms | 90' on center, typical (8 per block) | 1'* on center, typical |
| pedestrian-scale lamps | 110' on center, typical (6 per block) | 1'* on center, typical |

| FURNITURE | SPACING | LOCATION |
| --- | --- | --- |
| benches | varies (4 per block typical) | 2'* on center, typical |
| trash receptacles | varies (6 per block typical) | 2'* on center, typical |
| newsracks | 16 per block; groups of 4 typical | 2'* on center, typical |

| IMAGES | | |
| --- | --- | --- |
| adaptive reuse of historic buildings | valet parking at sidewalk | wide street: 2 parking aisles, 4 travel lanes, and 1 left-turn lane |

**\*Dimension from Back of Curb**

# PLAN, SECTION, AND DETAIL

Although the right-of-way is nearly 100 feet wide, pedestrian activity occurs at significant levels throughout the district. A dedicated left turn lane pocket in the middle of the street maintains traffic speeds at a significant level along the street, however "scramble" crosswalks located along Colorado Boulevard mitigate the traffic flows by encouraging diagonal pedestrian movements at key intersections. There are high-quality pedestrian linkages to Colorado Boulevard from perimeter parking locations. Street furniture and signage is of exceptionally high quality, but the street trees are currently undersized and tend to provide inadequate shade.

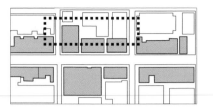

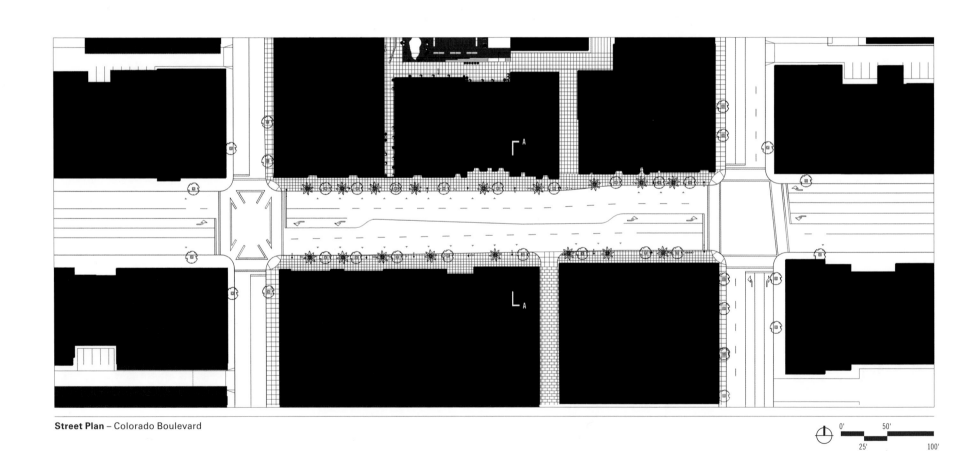

**Street Plan** – Colorado Boulevard

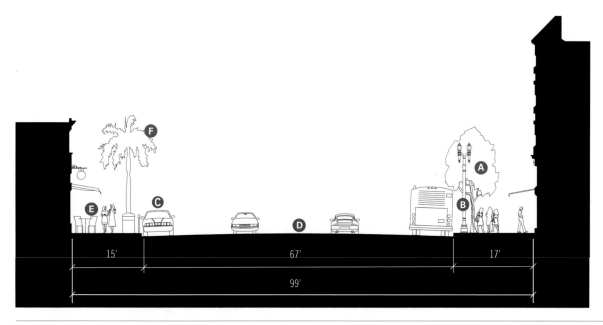

**Street Section AA** – Colorado Boulevard

15'  67'  17'

99'

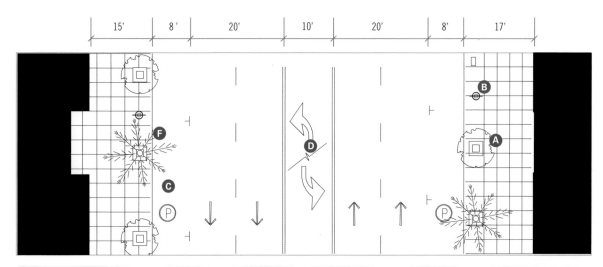

15'  8'  20'  10'  20'  8'  17'

**Plan Detail** – Colorado Boulevard

0'  5'  10'  20'

**A** Street Tree: Ginkgo

**B** Lamppost

**C** Parking Lane

**D** Left-Turn Lane

**E** Outdoor Dining

**F** Street Tree: Queen Palm

# RODEO DRIVE

## Beverly Hills, California

Rodeo Drive has a wide, landscaped median, midblock pedestrian crossings, and generous sidewalks. Although the street contains two travel lanes in opposite directions, vehicular traffic along Rodeo is notably slower than the traffic on streets of comparable scale; this is mostly due to midblock pedestrian crossings along the street. Rodeo is tenanted by many restaurants and luxury-goods retailers that sell apparel, jewelry, and home furnishings. Upper stories include limited creative office space. Parking is provided in a number of structures along Rodeo Drive that also house ground-floor retail space to maintain an uninterrupted shopping experience along the street.

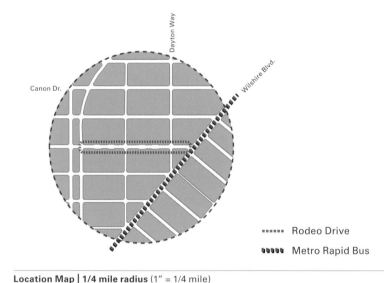

······ Rodeo Drive

▮▮▮▮▮ Metro Rapid Bus

**Location Map | 1/4 mile radius** (1″ = 1/4 mile)

**Figure Ground**

0'    300'
100'    600'

■ Apparel: 65%

■ Restaurant: 25%

■ Jewelry: 5%

■ Home Furnishings: 5%

**Land Use**

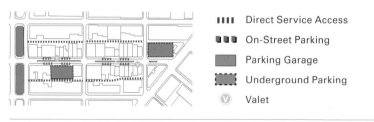

▮▮▮▮ Direct Service Access

▮▮▮ On-Street Parking

■ Parking Garage

▩ Underground Parking

Ⓥ Valet

**Parking and Servicing**

| STREET | DIMENSIONS | DESIGN |
| --- | --- | --- |
| building face-to-face | 96' ± | building setbacks vary between one and four feet |
| curb-to-curb | 50'-66' | varies to provide pockets of on-street parking |
| travel lanes | 4 @ 10' each typical | two travel lanes in each directions |
| median | 8' typical | landscaped median/left-turn pocket |
| parking lane | 8' typical | curbside pockets |
| sidewalk | 12'–20' | width varies depending on presence of street parking |
| curb height | 6" | |

| TREES | SPACING | LOCATION | PLANTING CONDITION | DESIGN |
| --- | --- | --- | --- | --- |
| royal palm *(roystonea)* | 30' on center, typical (36 per block) | 3' on center, typical | open bed | street trees |
| date palm *(phoenix dactylifera)* | 50' on center, typical (6 per block) | 4' on center, typical | open bed | median trees |
| small palms | 8' on center, typical (42 per block) | 4' on center, typical | open bed | median trees |

| LIGHTING | SPACING | LOCATION |
| --- | --- | --- |
| overhead with traffic control | end-of-block (2 per block) | 1'* on center, typical |
| overhead with banner arms | 75' on center, typical (8 per block) | 1'* on center, typical |

| FURNITURE | SPACING | LOCATION |
| --- | --- | --- |
| benches | varies (8 per block typical) | 1'* on center, typical |
| trash receptacles | 60' (6 per block typical) | 1'–7"* on center, typical |

| IMAGES | | |
| --- | --- | --- |
| prada store | landscape median | uncluttered sidewalks |

**\*Dimension from Back of Curb**

# PLAN, SECTION, AND DETAIL

The majority of streetscape elements are evenly spaced. Royal palms are planted along the sidewalks and spaced at 30-foot intervals; date palms are used along the median at 50-foot intervals. Public artwork on the median creates a unique identity. Benches, trash receptacles, and street lamps are placed sparingly along the sidewalk, allowing storefronts to remain highly visible.

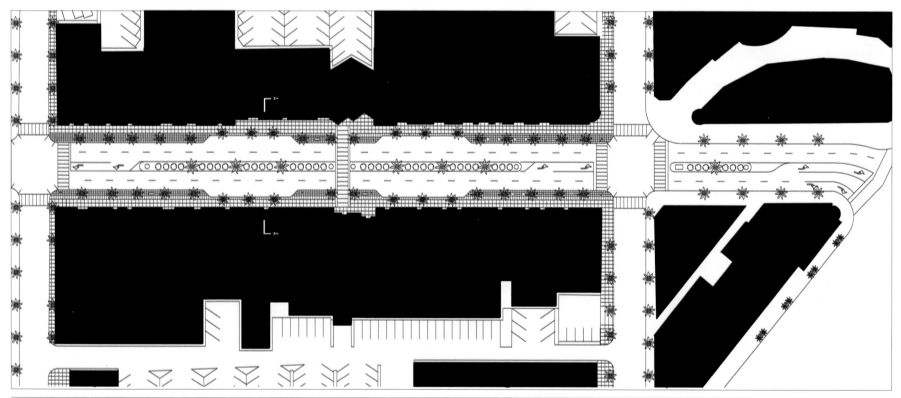

**Street Plan** – Rodeo Drive

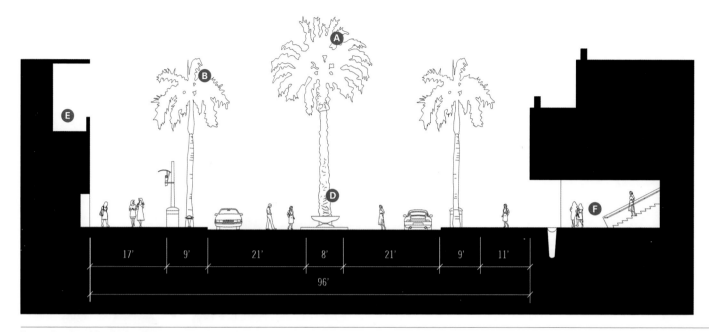

**Street Section AA** – Rodeo Drive

17'  9'  21'  8'  21'  9'  11'

96'

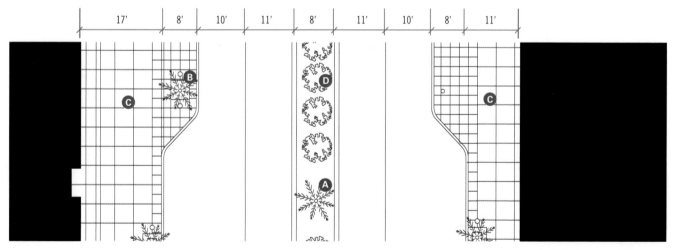

**Plan Detail** – Rodeo Drive

17'  8'  10'  11'  8'  11'  10'  8'  11'

Ⓐ Street Tree: Date Palm

Ⓑ Street Tree: Royal Palm

Ⓒ Widened Sidewalk

Ⓓ Landscape Median

Ⓔ Retail Balcony

Ⓕ Open-Air Store Entry (Prada)

0'   10'
5'        20'

# THIRD STREET PROMENADE

Santa Monica, California

Third Street Promenade is three blocks long and contains a mix of tourist-oriented shops, apparel stores, entertainment venues, and restaurants. Upper-level spaces include office, retail, and residential space. The promenade is closed to vehicular traffic by bollards located at Third Street's intersections with Wilshire, Arizona, Colorado, and Broadway. Pedestrians are able to move freely throughout the broad promenade on sidewalks and median areas, which can be accessed by service vehicles only for loading, street cleaning, and event setup during off-hours. Service alleys and parking structures are located parallel to Third Street along Second and Fourth streets.

**Figure Ground**

0' 100' 300' 600'

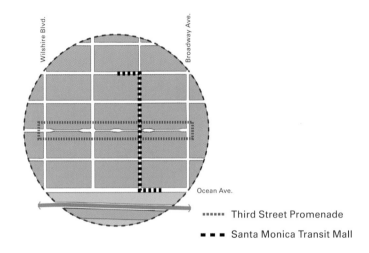

**Location Map | 1/4 mile radius** (1" = 1/4 mile)

■■■■■ Third Street Promenade

■ ■ ■ Santa Monica Transit Mall

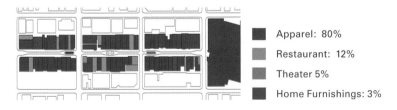

**Land Use**

■ Apparel: 80%

■ Restaurant: 12%

■ Theater 5%

■ Home Furnishings: 3%

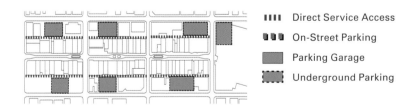

**Parking and Servicing**

▮▮▮▮ Direct Service Access

▮ ▮ ▮ On-Street Parking

■ Parking Garage

▨ Underground Parking

| STREET | DIMENSIONS | DESIGN |
|---|---|---|
| building face-to-face | 80' ± | variable setbacks provide room for outdoor dining |
| curb-to-curb | 20'–48' | width increases at intersections and midblock to accomodate median |
| travel lanes | none | |
| median | 22' | located at intersections and midblock |
| parking lane | none | |
| sidewalk | 12'–24' ± | width widens at curb bumpouts |
| curb height | 3" | |

| TREES | SPACING | LOCATION | PLANTING CONDITION | DESIGN |
|---|---|---|---|---|
| mexican fan palm *(washingtonia robusta)* | 28' on center, typical (24 per block) | 10' on center, typical | open bed | street trees |
| jacaranda *(jacaranda mimosifolia)* | 16' on center, typical (28 per block) | 2' on center, typical | decorative grate | street trees |

| LIGHTING | SPACING | LOCATION |
|---|---|---|
| overhead with traffic control | end-of-block (2 per block) | 1'* on center, typical |
| overhead with banner arms | 75' on center, typical (8 per block) | 1'* on center, typical |

| FURNITURE | SPACING | LOCATION |
|---|---|---|
| benches | varies (12 per block typical) | 6'* on center, typical |
| kiosks | varies (16 per block) | 2'* typical |

| IMAGES | | |
|---|---|---|
| elaborate streetscape | mostly national retailers | topiary median |

**\*Dimension from Back of Curb**

# PLAN, SECTION, AND DETAIL

Streetscape elements are evenly spaced. Decorative paving lines the sidewalk's edge and crosses from curb to curb every 50 feet. Fan palms are spaced at regular intervals along the promenade, with smaller, evenly spaced shade trees along the sidewalk edge. Street lamps with banner arms are also found along the promenade's sidewalk. Curbs are three inches tall, making it easy for pedestrians to cross from one side of the street to the other.

There are pavilions at intersections that house convenience retail and dining areas. Topiary fountains are located in the middle and at the ends of the blocks along the promenade.

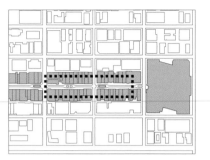

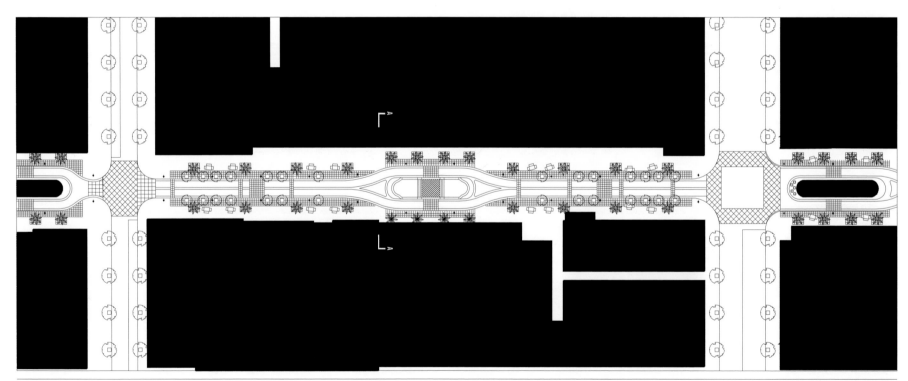

**Street Plan –** Third Street Promenade

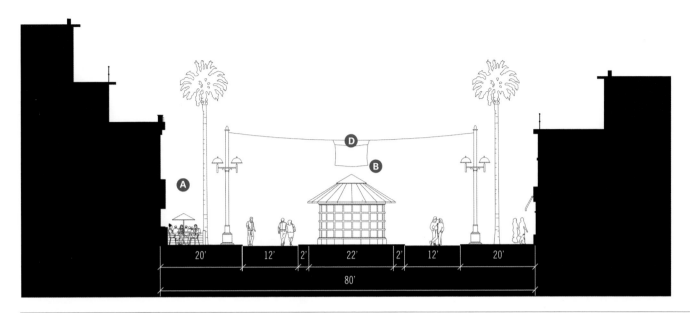

**Street Section AA** – Third Street Promenade

20' | 12' | 2' | 22' | 2' | 12' | 20'

80'

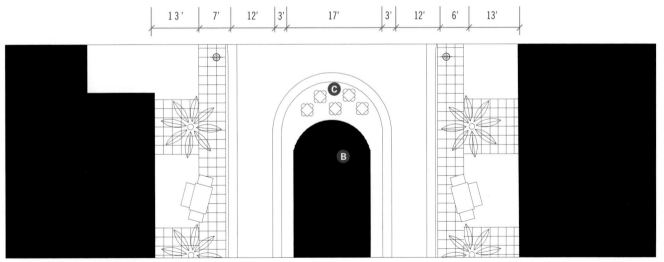

13' | 7' | 12' | 3' | 17' | 3' | 12' | 6' | 13'

**Plan Detail** – Third Street Promenade

**A** Outdoor Dining

**B** Retail Pavilion

**C** Outdoor Seating

**D** Overhead Banner

0' | 10'

5' | 20'

# VENICE BOARDWALK
## Venice, California

Venice Boardwalk offers a mix of retail, services, and dining catering mostly to tourists visiting the area. Windward Avenue is lined by multistory structures with arcaded, ground-floor retail space and limited creative office and hotel space on upper stories. The pedestrian boardwalk contains small-scale retail and kiosks run by local artisans. Adjacent to the boardwalk is an expansive recreation area containing courts for basketball and tennis, as well as seating areas. Speedway, an access road that runs parallel to the boardwalk, provides parking and service access.

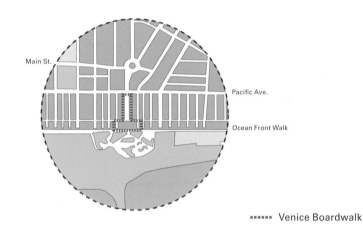

Main St.

Pacific Ave.

Ocean Front Walk

······ Venice Boardwalk

**Location Map | 1/4 mile radius** (1″ = 1/4 mile)

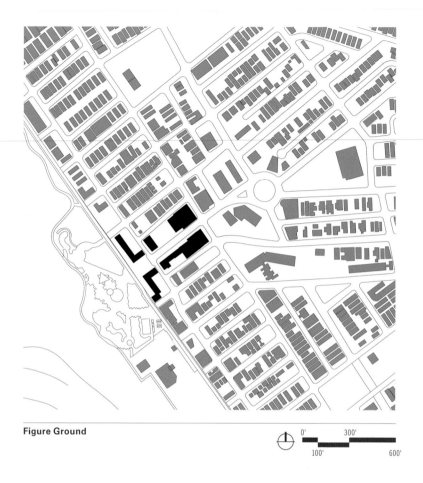

**Figure Ground**

0'    300'
100'    600'

**Land Use**

■ Apparel: 53%
■ Restaurant: 23%
■ Youth Hostel 10%
□ Residential: 10%
□ Tatoo Parlor: 4%

**Parking and Servicing**

▮▮▮▮ Direct Service Access
▮▮▮ On-Street Parking
▮ Parking Garage

| STREET | DIMENSIONS | DESIGN |
|---|---|---|
| building face-to-face | 82' ± | building setbacks vary between one and three feet |
| curb-to-curb | 60' | curb line tapers at intersection approach to accommodate right-turn lane |
| travel lanes | 2 @ 16' each | lane provides room to overtake vehicles waiting to park |
| median | none | located at intersections and midblock |
| parking lane | 14' (angled) | |
| sidewalk | 11'–14' ± | partially arcade |
| curb height | 5" | |

| TREES | SPACING | LOCATION | PLANTING CONDITION | DESIGN |
|---|---|---|---|---|
| none | | | | |

| LIGHTING | SPACING | LOCATION |
|---|---|---|
| overhead with traffic control | varies (26 per block typ.) | 1'* on center, typical |
| overhead with banner arms | 75' on center, typical (8 per block) | 1'* on center, typical |

| FURNITURE | SPACING | LOCATION |
|---|---|---|
| trash receptacles | 30' on center, typical | 2'* on center, typical |

| IMAGES | | |
|---|---|---|
| arcade sidewalk | temporary sidewalk displays | angled parking |

**\*Dimension from Back of Curb**

# PLAN, SECTION, AND DETAIL

Windward Avenue contains angled street parking from Pacific Avenue to Speedway. Along Windward, the pedestrian arcades offer shaded passage. To the west of Speedway, Windward transitions into a pedestrian plaza that feeds into the boardwalk. An informal boundary exists between storefronts and the boardwalk, which allows for retail displays to spill out into the pedestrian right-of-way.

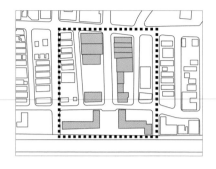

**Street Plan** – Venice Boardwalk

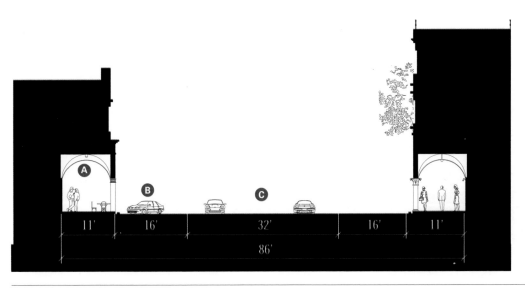
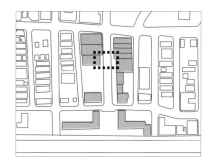

**Street Section AA** – St. Marks Place

11'  16'  32'  16'  11'

86'

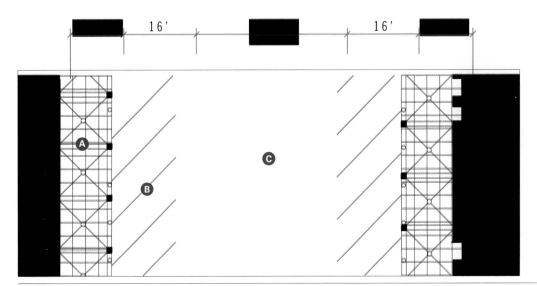

16'  16'

**Plan Detail** – St. Marks Place

Ⓐ Arcaded Sidewalks

Ⓑ Angled Parking

Ⓒ Windward Avenue

0'  10'

5'  20'

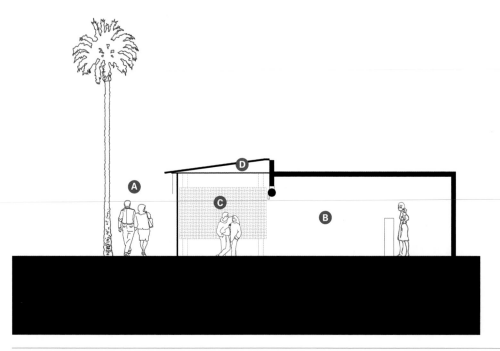

**Street Section BB** – Boardwalk Kiosks

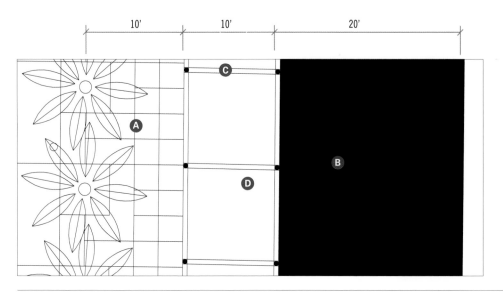

**Street Plan** – Boardwalk Kiosks

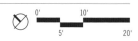

Ⓐ Boardwalk

Ⓑ Shipping containers with Roll-up Doors

Ⓒ Side wall display

Ⓓ Canopy Shade

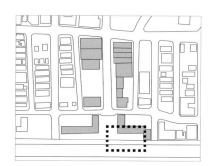

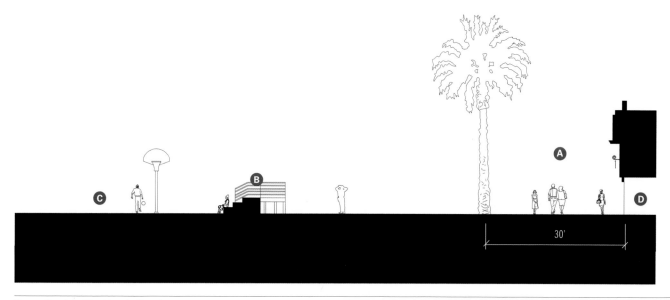

**Street Section CC** – Muscle Beach

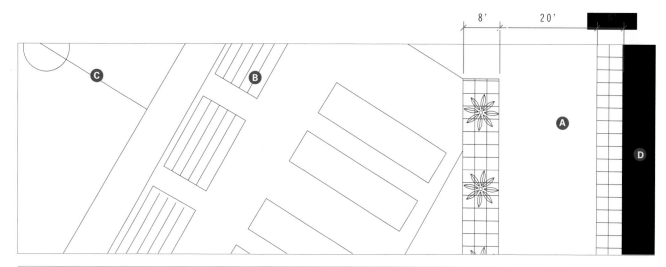

**Plan Detail** – Muscle Beach

Ⓐ Boardwalk

Ⓑ Step Seating

Ⓒ Basketball Court

Ⓓ Retail with Roll-up Doors

### The relationship of street to arterial routes

Typically, shopping streets are located perpendicular or parallel to an arterial road, but rarely are they arterials themselves. The automobile traffic on an arterial is incompatible with the pedestrian activity along a shopping street. Colorado Boulevard in Pasadena, California, is an exception to this rule and mitigates the impact of its arterial traffic through use of high-volume pedestrian crossings at key intersections.

### Travel Lane Width

Shopping streets often have one or two travel lanes going each way and generally do not have a dedicated left-turn lane, although left turns are generally permitted. This allows the street to remain as narrow as possible to encourage wide sidewalks and pedestrian cross-shopping, while maintaining traffic volume.

### Building relationship to property line

Buildings on the shopping streets we studied are generally built near or on the property line, with flat façades and punched openings. The best streets have about 80 to 85 percent enclosure/adherence to the property line. Overhead encroachments such as awnings, signs, and balconies reinforce the "address" of the street. The distance between buildings across the street from each other varies between 65 and 90 feet. The maximum recommended dimension from building face to building face is about 100 feet.

### On-Street Parking

On-street parking is a must for a shopping street. It is convenient for shoppers and shop owners alike. It works to slow down traffic and make the street more active with pedestrians. Parallel parking is the most common arrangement; it narrows the roadbed, thereby narrowing the overall dimension of the street. Another popular option is angled parking, which additionally widens the street because of the space required to back vehicles out of spots into oncoming traffic. One way of mitigating this effect is to configure one side of the street with angled parking, one with parallel. Head-in parking along shopping streets is discouraged.

### Bulbouts

Bulbouts are often used at major intersections to make the street easier for pedestrian crossing. Coupled with other pedestrian accommodations such as "zero curbs" (where the curb is flat to the street), bulbouts can create a high-quality walking environment.

### Block Size

Blocks fewer than 200 feet long have difficulty accommodating the amount of parking and car access necessary to support a mixed use and/or retail program. Blocks longer than 500 feet are difficult to traverse by foot and require midblock breaks to work effectively at promoting pedestrian activity. As a rule of thumb, the most workable blocks for shopping activities tend to be between two and four acres in size.

### Sidewalks

Zone 1 is located along the storefront and contains storefront entries, signage and awnings, outdoor dining, and movable planters.

Zone 2, located in the middle of sidewalk, is a flexible strolling area, which in some instances can contain public art or signage that appeal to pedestrians.

Zone 3 is at curb level and contains street trees, planting areas, benches, trash cans, and streetlights.

A typical retail sidewalk is between 12 and 25 feet wide from curb to building face. There are effective examples (Ocean Drive in South Beach, Florida) where zone 1's dining component is integrated into an expanded zone 3 adjacent to the street curb. This adds an interesting additional social dynamic to zone 2 (waiters intermingling with pedestrians passing between the building and the dining areas along the street), but the arrangement is not typical.

Section Five

# PLACES

The urban environment is enhanced through the careful placement of discrete outdoor spaces that are smaller than squares, greens, and parks. Despite their relatively small size, we often find that these spaces are the heart of successful active mixed use developments. Places can be successfully designed to accommodate a wide variety of activities, from solitary rest and contemplation to high levels of social interaction and movement.

As we did in our study of shopping streets, we focused on popular places in greater Los Angeles. Some of these places, such as The Grove and L.A. Live, are of recent origin but have attracted the attention of national media and large numbers of visitors. Edgemar is neighborhood place used mostly by locals.

This study relies on detailed plan and section drawings based on aerial imagery, site reconnaissance, and field measurements.

# SPATIAL ENCLOSURE / PLACE DIMENSIONS

The places we studied have a consistent ratio of enclosure that ranges from 1:2 to 1:4, despite the significant variation in their relative size. Via Rodeo is an exception that is more like a passage, with a spatial enclosure ratio of 1:1. Higher ratios of enclosure can be found, but lower than 1:4 is not recommended.

### Ratio of Enclosure

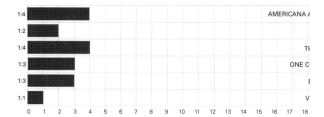

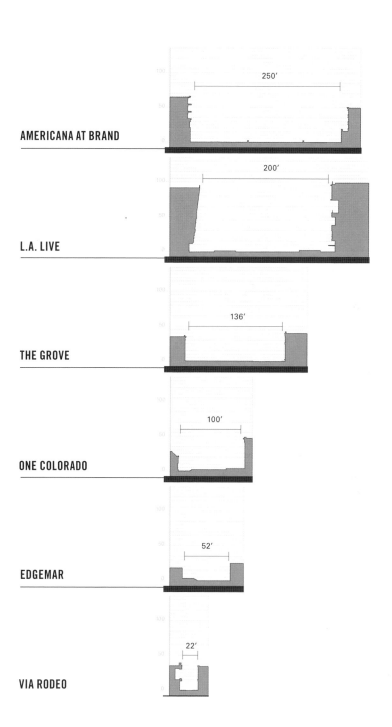

AMERICANA AT BRAND — 250'

L.A. LIVE — 200'

THE GROVE — 136'

ONE COLORADO — 100'

EDGEMAR — 52'

VIA RODEO — 22'

# PLACES SCALE COMPARISON

**AMERICANA AT BRAND**
Glendale, California

**EDGEMAR**
Santa Monica, California

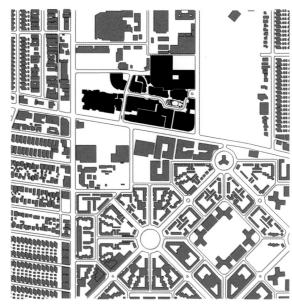

**THE GROVE**
Los Angeles

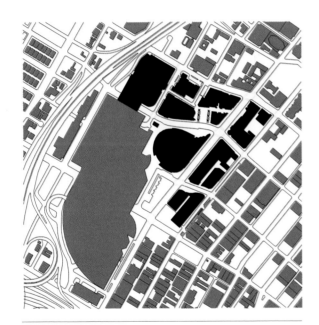

**L.A. LIVE**
Los Angeles

**ONE COLORADO**
Pasadena, California

**VIA RODEO**
Beverly Hills, California

# AMERICANA AT BRAND

Glendale, California

Americana at Brand, an infill project that opened in 2008, consists of retail, dining, upper-story residential space, and limited office space. The primary anchors are an 18-screen cinema and a multistory bookstore. The centerpiece of Americana at Brand is a large grass lawn bounded by shops, outdoor dining, and a streetcar line. This space is accented by a two-tiered water feature, a "tot lot," and various retail kiosks. A multilevel parking deck is located along the northern edge of the property and is screened by mixed use structures accessible by a distinctive elevator tower.

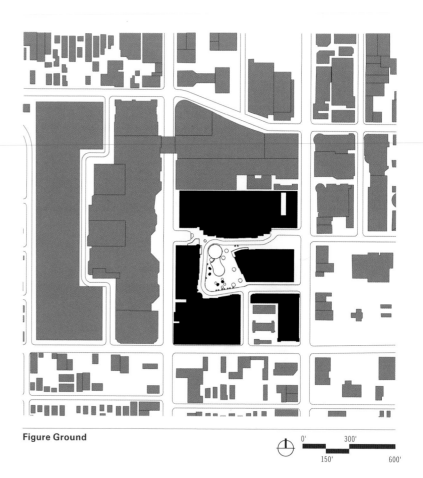

**Figure Ground**

0'   150'   300'   600'

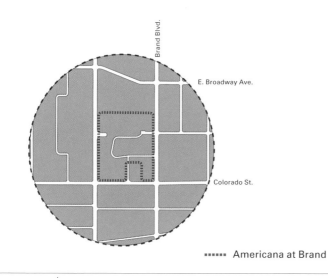

······ Americana at Brand

**Location Map | 1/4 mile radius** (1″ = 1/4 mile)

■ Apparel: 44%
■ Restaurant: 10%
■ Cinema: 24%
■ Other Retail: 14%
■ Residential: 5%
■ Home Furnishings: 3%

**Land Use**

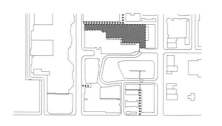

▪▪▪▪▪ Interior Service Access
▮▮▮▮ Direct Service Access
▨ Parking Garage
Ⓥ Valet

**Parking and Servicing**

| PLAZA | AREA | LENGTH | WIDTH | IMAGES |
|---|---|---|---|---|
| dimensions | 110,500 ± sq ft | 370' ± | 250' ± | |

elevator tower attached to major parking deck

| GROUND TREATMENT | DESIGN | AREA | AREA BREAKDOWN |
|---|---|---|---|
| sidewalk paving | 5' x 5' stone pavers | 32,700 ± square feet | 30% |
| specialty stone | varing stone pavers | 9,000 ± square feet | 8% |
| street paving | 26' wide blacktop | 17,600 ± square feet | 16% |
| trolley right-of-way | 9' teak planking | 3,200 ± square feet | 3% |
| lawn | | 21,750 ± square feet | 20% |
| tot lot | | 1,350 ± square feet | 1% |
| water feature | pool with fountains and spillway | 12,600 ± square feet | 11% |

| TREES | QUANTITY | SPACING | LOCATION | PLANTING CONDITION |
|---|---|---|---|---|
| street trees | 37 | 40' on center, typical | along street | 5' x 8' and 4' x 4' curbside beds |
| lawn trees | 11 | 60' on center, typical | within lawn / paving | within floral bed / paving |
| total | 48 | | | total planting ratio: 1/2300± square feet |

high-quality streetscape

| LIGHTING | QUANTITY | SPACING | LOCATION | |
|---|---|---|---|---|
| street lamps | 20 | 50' on center, typical | 1' *on center, typical | |
| string lights | 8 | 20' | above open dining | |
| total | 28 | | | total lighting ratio: 1/4,000 ± square feet |

| SEATING | QUANTITY | LOCATION | RATIO |
|---|---|---|---|
| benches | 17 | streetside | 1/750 ± square feet |
| patios | 4,900 ± square feet (4% of total plaza area) | | |
| open dining | 6 (tables for 2 or 4) | along lawn and tot lot | 2,150 ± square feet (2% of total plaza area) |
| street-side dining | 18 (tables for 4) | within streetscape | 6,100 ± square feet |

residential balconies overlooking street

**\*Dimension from Back of Curb**

# PLAN AND SECTION

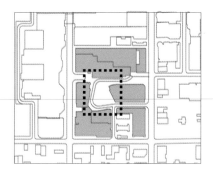

**Plaza Plan** – Americana at Brand

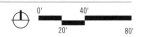

0'  40'
20'  80'

**Plaza Section AA** – Americana at Brand

- Ⓐ Great Lawn
- Ⓑ Water Feature
- Ⓒ Trolley Line
- Ⓓ Outdoor Dining
- Ⓔ Canopy Shade Tree
- Ⓕ Tot Lot
- Ⓖ Retail Pavilions
- Ⓗ Public Art

# EDGEMAR

Santa Monica, California

Edgemar is a unique mixed use development containing galleries, performance spaces, shops, offices, restaurants, outdoor seating, and a water feature. Originally a dairy, the property was refashioned in the 1980s as an arts district. While Edgemar's form, architecture, and materials palette are contemporary, the design and scale of the plaza are classically proportioned. Pedestrians enter through one of several passages from the street. Current tenants at Edgemar include a variety of arts-oriented retailers, a beauty salon, an architecture studio, a coffee shop, and the Edgemar Center for the Arts.

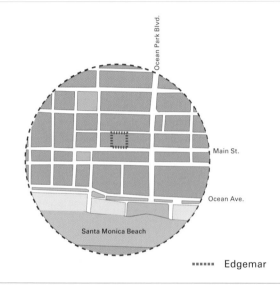

······ Edgemar

**Location Map | 1/4 mile radius** (1″ = 1/4 mile)

**Figure Ground**

- Theater / Gallery: 30%
- Professional Services: 25%
- Restaurant: 20%
- Home Furnishings: 12%
- Apparel: 8%
- Other Retail: 5%

**Land Use**

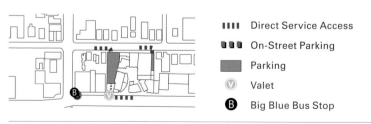

- **||||** Direct Service Access
- **▮▮▮** On-Street Parking
- ▮ Parking
- Ⓥ Valet
- Ⓑ Big Blue Bus Stop

**Parking and Servicing**

| PLAZA | AREA | LENGTH | WIDTH | IMAGES |
|---|---|---|---|---|
| | 4,000 ± square feet | 80' ± | 52' ± | |

| GROUND TREATMENT | DESIGN | AREA | AREA BREAKDOWN |
|---|---|---|---|
| plaza paving | 8' x 7' scoring pattern | 3,200 ± square feet | 80% |
| entryway paving | 6' x 7' angled scoring | 800 ± square feet | 20% |

| TREES | QUANTITY | SPACING | LOCATION PLANTING CONDITION |
|---|---|---|---|
| eucalyptus trees *(eucalyptus)* | 2 | 5' on center, typical, eastern side of plaza | decorative grate |
| total | 2 | total planting ratio: 1/2,000 ± square feet | |

street view

interior court

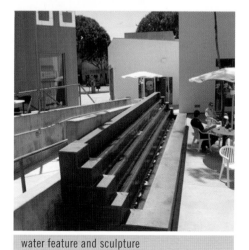

water feature and sculpture

**\*Dimension from Back of Curb**

# PLAN AND SECTION

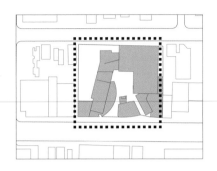

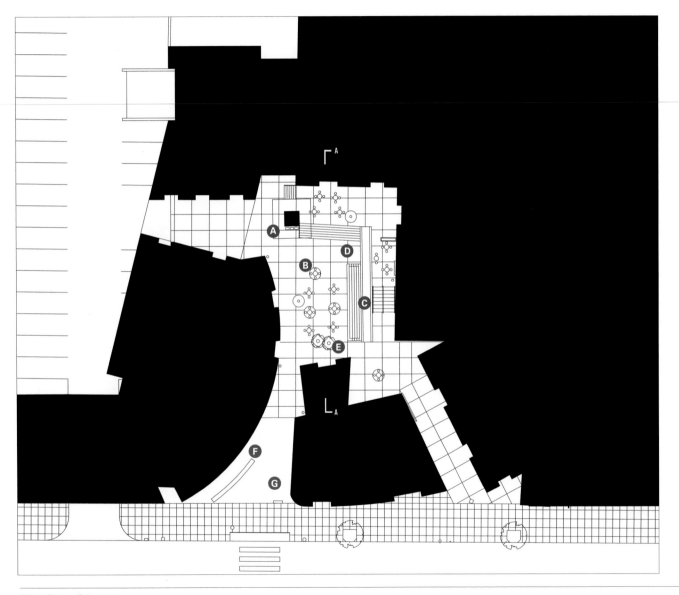

**Plaza Plan** – Edgemar

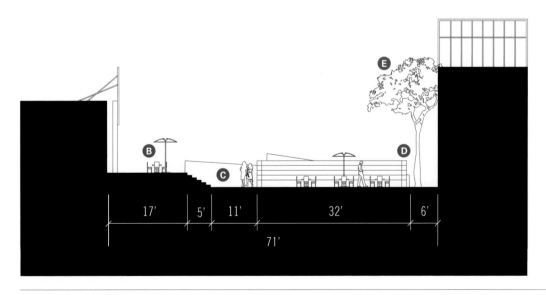

**Plaza Section AA** – Edgemar

- **A** Elevator
- **B** Outdoor Dining
- **C** Pedestrian Ramp
- **D** Water Feature
- **E** Canopy Tree
- **F** Bench Seating
- **G** Way Finding

0'  5'  10'  20'

# THE GROVE

Los Angeles

The Grove is an upscale shopping and dining district surrounded by residential space, offices, and museums. Pedestrians can walk down the central street or ride a streetcar, which runs on tracks in the street's center. The central gathering space located at the eastern side of the development consists of an open lawn, fountain, and a paved plaza with food kiosks and outdoor seating. Street trees are evenly spaced and flank movable retail kiosks and decorative street lamps.

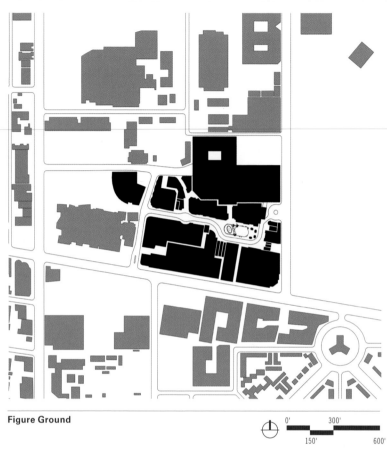

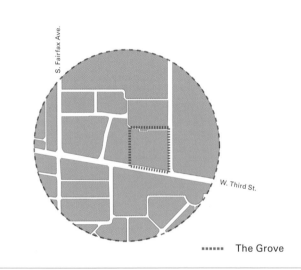

⋯⋯ The Grove

**Location Map | 1/4 mile radius** (1" = 1/4 mile)

**Figure Ground**

0'    300'
150'    600'

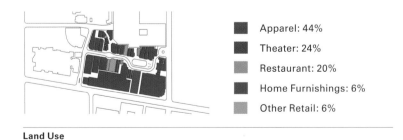

- ■ Apparel: 44%
- ■ Theater: 24%
- ■ Restaurant: 20%
- ■ Home Furnishings: 6%
- ■ Other Retail: 6%

**Land Use**

- ⋯⋯ Interior Service Access
- ⅠⅠⅠⅠ Direct Service Access
- ⬚ Parking Garage
- Ⓥ Valet

**Parking and Servicing**

| PLAZA | AREA | LENGTH | WIDTH | IMAGES |
|---|---|---|---|---|
| dimensions | 45,000 ± square feet | 314' ± | 136' ± | |

| GROUND TREATMENT | DESIGN | AREA | AREA BREAKDOWN | |
|---|---|---|---|---|
| sidewalk paving | 3' x 3' stone pavers | 18,000 ± square feet | 40% | |
| specialty stone | varing stone pavers | 5,000 ± square feet | 11% | |
| street paving | 26' wide blacktop | 11,000± square feet | 25% | |
| trolley right-of-way | 9' wide brick pattern | 5,000 ± square feet | 11% | |
| lawn | | 4,000 ± square feet | 8% | |
| water feature | pool with fountains | 2,000 ± square feet | 5% | high quality streetscape |

| TREES | QUANTITY | SPACING | LOCATION | PLANTING CONDITION | |
|---|---|---|---|---|---|
| street trees | 12 | 55' on center, typical | along street | 5' x 8' curbside beds | |
| coral tree (erythrina indica) | 3 | 25' on center, typical | grouped around walkway | open lawn | |
| italian spruce (cupressus sempervirens) | 8 | 25' on center, typical | along fountain railing | | |
| small palms | 7 | | around store entries | 4' x 4' planters | |
| total: | 30 | | | total planting ratio: 1/1500 ± square feet | greenspace |

| LIGHTING | QUANTITY | SPACING | LOCATION | |
|---|---|---|---|---|
| street lamps | 15 | 50' on center, typical | 1' *on center, typical | |
| total: | 15 | | | total lighting ratio: 1/3,000 ± square feet |

| SEATING | QUANTITY | LOCATION | RATIO |
|---|---|---|---|
| benches | 6 | along edge of lawn | 1/750 ± square feet |
| restaurant dinning | 16 (tables for 4) | restaurant patios | 950 ± square feet (2% of total plaza area) |
| open dining | 12 (tables for 4) | parkside court | 1,500 ± square feet (3% of total plaza area) |
| streetside dining | 6 (tables for 3) | within street amenity space | 1/7,500 ± square feet |

mature trees

**\*Dimension from Back of Curb**

# PLAN AND SECTION

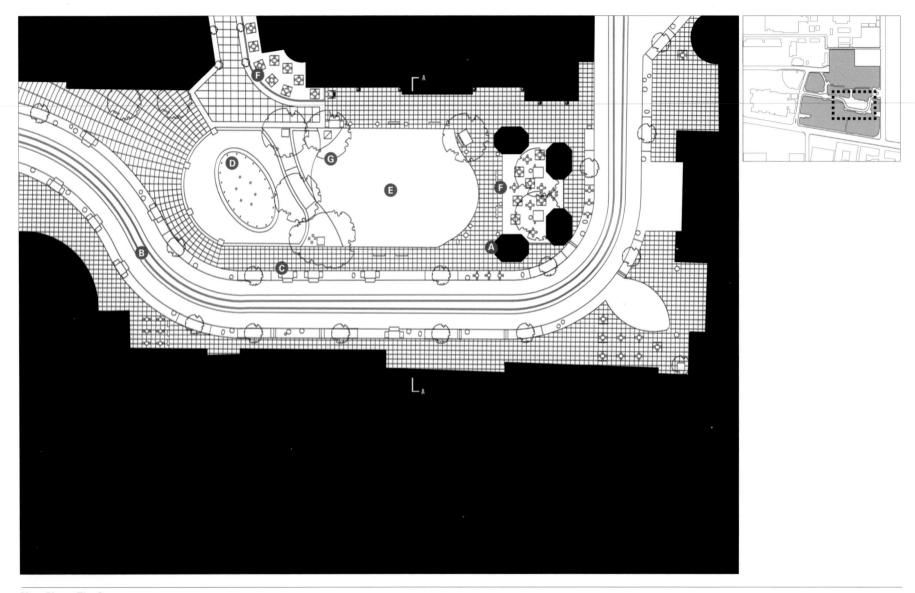

**Plaza Plan** – The Grove

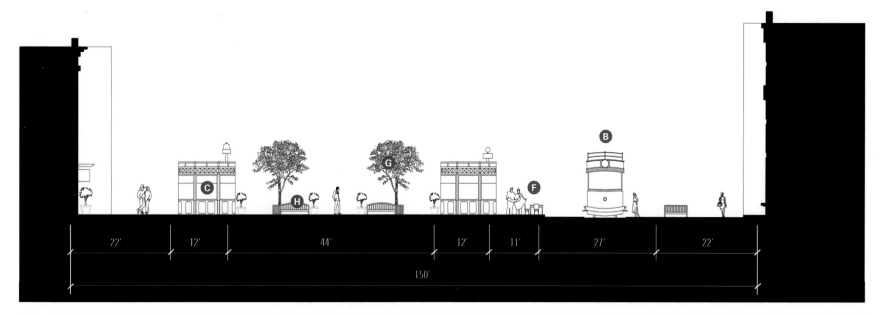

A Retail Kiosk
B Trolley Line
C Kiosk
D Water Feature
E Central Lawn
F Outdoor Dining
G Canopy Shade Trees
H Outdoor Seating

**Plaza Section AA** – The Grove

# L.A. LIVE
## Los Angeles

L.A. Live was designed to become the new central entertainment hub of downtown Los Angeles. It includes Staples Arena (home of the Los Angeles Lakers, Clippers, Kings, and Sparks), the newly expanded L.A. Convention Center and Hotel, the 6,500-seat Nokia theater, restaurants, ESPN's West Coast broadcast facilities, Club Nokia, the Grammy museum, 150,000 gross square feet of office space, a bowling alley, 800 residential units, and 300,000 square feet of retail, health, and fitness space. The entire back façade facing the plaza is made of low- and high-definition LED screens. The project is best experienced during a major event, where the energy of the people on the street matches the visual spectacle of the buildings and signs around them.

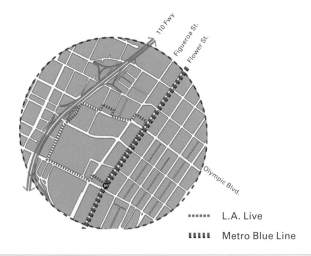

┈┈┈┈  L.A. Live

▮▮▮▮  Metro Blue Line

**Location Map | 1/4 mile radius** (1″ = 1/4 mile)

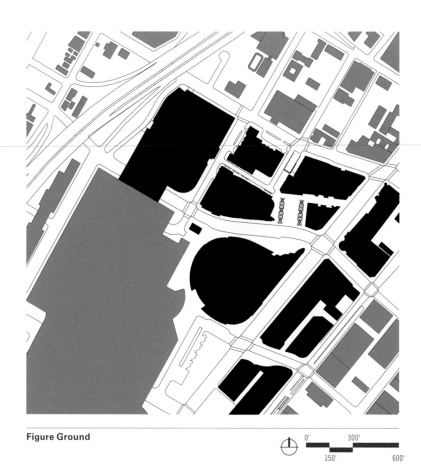

**Figure Ground**

0'    300'
150'    600'

**Land Use**

■ Entertainment / Meeting: 35%

▨ Residential: 22%

■ Hotel: 16%

■ Apparel: 15%

■ Restaurant: 10%

■ Cinema: 2%

**Parking and Servicing**

▮▮▮▮  Direct Service Access

▮▮▮  On-Street Parking

▮  Parking

Ⓥ  Valet

| PLAZA | AREA | LENGTH | WIDTH | | IMAGES |
|---|---|---|---|---|---|
| dimensions | 32,000 ± square feet | 160' ± | 200' ± | | |

| GROUND TREATMENT | DESIGN | AREA | AREA BREAKDOWN |
|---|---|---|---|
| special plaza and road paving | 2' x 12' pavers | 25,000 ± square feet | 80% |
| plaza paving | 8' x 8' scoring pattern | 7,000 ± square feet | 20% |

| TREES | QUANTITY | SPACING | LOCATION | PLANTING CONDITION |
|---|---|---|---|---|
| canopy trees | 24 10' on center, typical | 8' from building face | raised planters | |
| total: | 24 | | total planting ratio: 1/1,500± square feet | |

view of the plaza from street level

| LIGHTING | QUANTITY | SPACING | LOCATION |
|---|---|---|---|
| light towers | 6 | 60' on center, typical | raised planters. |
| total: | 6 | | total lighting ratio: 1/5,000± square feet |

landscape feature

passage between ESPN and office building

**\*Dimension from Back of Curb**

# PLAN AND SECTION

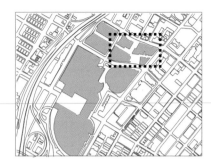

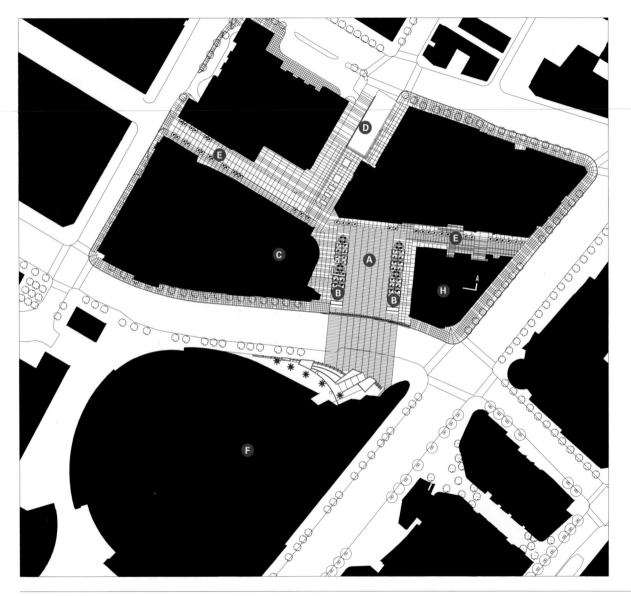

**Plaza Plan** – L.A. Live

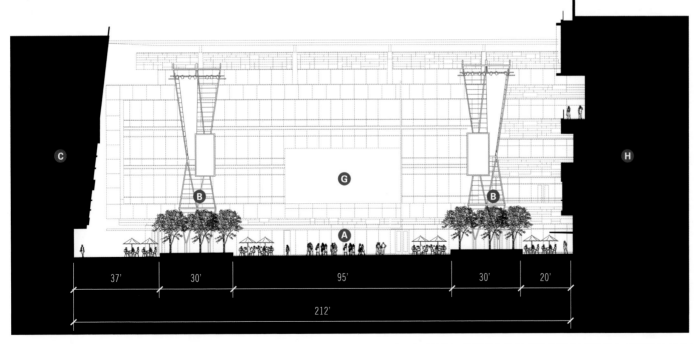

37'  30'  95'  30'  20'

212'

**A** Central Plaza

**B** Raised Planters/Light Towers

**C** Nokia Theater

**D** Vehicular Alley/Garage Access

**E** Pedestrian Alley

**F** Staples Center

**G** Video Screen

**H** ESPN Broadcast Facility

**Plaza Section AA** – L.A. Live

0'    20'
10'         40'

# ONE COLORADO

Pasadena, California

One Colorado is known for its eclectic mix of contemporary retail and dining within the city's historic buildings. Pedestrians enter One Colorado through a series of historic alleyways, which have been retrofitted with decorative pavers, planters, and light fixtures. The central plaza is an outdoor dining space for several restaurants and a venue for a variety of community arts, culture, and civic events. Metal framed planter boxes are used to define areas for various activities in the plaza and can be moved to accommodate different outdoor events throughout the year.

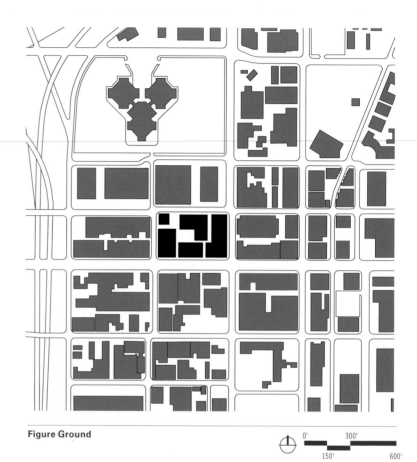

**Figure Ground**

0'   150'   300'   600'

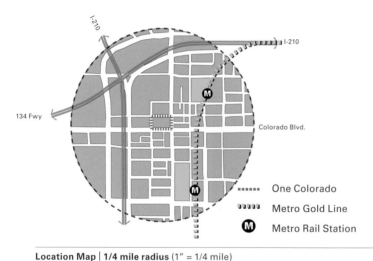

- One Colorado
- Metro Gold Line
- Ⓜ Metro Rail Station

**Location Map | 1/4 mile radius (1″ = 1/4 mile)**

**Land Use**

- Apparel: 50%
- Restaurant: 29%
- Home Furnishings: 13%
- Cinema: 8%

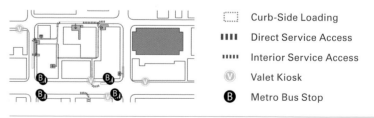

**Parking and Servicing**

- Curb-Side Loading
- Direct Service Access
- Interior Service Access
- Ⓥ Valet Kiosk
- Ⓑ Metro Bus Stop

| PLAZA | AREA | LENGTH | WIDTH | IMAGES |
|---|---|---|---|---|
| dimensions | 14,000 ± square feet | 140' ± | 100' ± | |

| GROUND TREATMENT | DESIGN | AREA | AREA BREAKDOWN | |
|---|---|---|---|---|
| plaza paving | herringbone brick pattern | 7,000 ± square feet | 52% | |
| alley paving | 3' x 4' stone pavers | 5,000 ± square feet | 34% | |
| patio paving | 3' x 3' scoring pattern | 2,000± square feet | 14% | event space |

| TREES | QUANTITY | SPACING | LOCATION | PLANTING CONDITION |
|---|---|---|---|---|
| small planted trees | 22 | 20' on center, typical | aligning alley and plaza | 3' diameter stone planters |
| small planted palms | 50 | 30' on center, typical | aligning alley and plaza | 3' x 3' stone planters |
| chinese elm (ulmus parvifolia) | 18 | 12' on center, typical | around central dining area | 2' x 12' iron planters |
| total | 90 | | | total planting ratio: 1/155± square feet |

| LIGHTING | QUANTITY | SPACING | LOCATION | |
|---|---|---|---|---|
| wall-mounted | 52 | 20' on center, typical | building side | |
| utility | 1 | | southwest corner of plaza | |
| balcony lamps | 5 | 18' on center, typical | balcony railing | |
| total | 58 | | | total lighting ratio: 1/250 ± square feet |

paseo connections

| SEATING | QUANTITY | LOCATION | RATIO |
|---|---|---|---|
| benches | 4 | plaza perimeter | 1/750 ± square feet |
| open dining | 8 (tables for 4) | plaza center | 1,500 ± square feet (10% of total plaza area) |
| restaurant dining | 42 (tables for 4) | dining patios | 2,000 ± square feet (14% of total plaza area) |

high-quality details

**\*Dimension from Back of Curb**

# PLAN AND SECTION

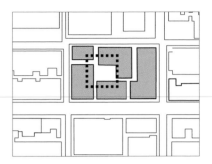

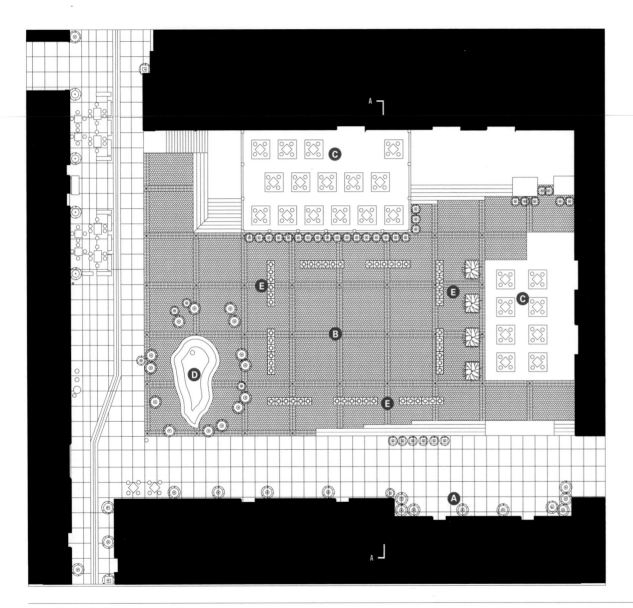

**Plaza Plan** – One Colorado

0'    5'    15'    25'

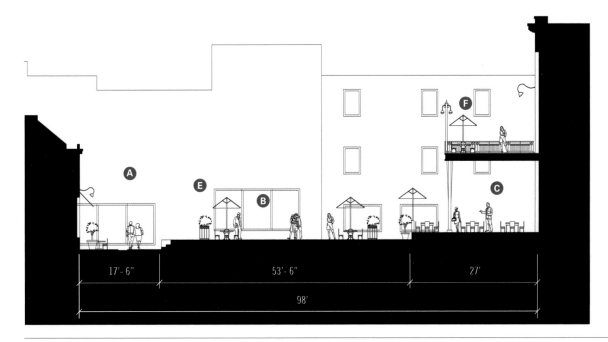

17'- 6"    53'- 6"    27'

98'

**A** Alley

**B** Central Plaza

**C** Outdoor Seating

**D** Water Feature

**E** Planters

**F** Dining Terrace

**Plaza Section AA** – One Colorado

# VIA RODEO

Beverly Hills, California

Located at the Wilshire Boulevard entry to Rodeo Drive, Via Rodeo is an especially compact urban block offering a mix of restaurants, salons, and shops. Running through the center of the block is a European-scale pedestrian passage featuring stone street pavers, decorative street lamps, planters, and steps leading to a fountain. Parking is provided in an underground structure, which can be accessed along Dayton Way. The Via itself is only 34 feet wide at its widest point, and in some places it is 22 feet wide. Pedestrians enter the Via through two entrances: one at grade, located at the intersection of Rodeo Drive and Dayton Way. From the north, the pedestrian enters at street level. The Via then gently slopes up, turns, and to the viewer's surprise ends one level above the street, with a grand stairway back down to street level. Two restaurants with outdoor dining spaces overlook the grand staircase and fountain.

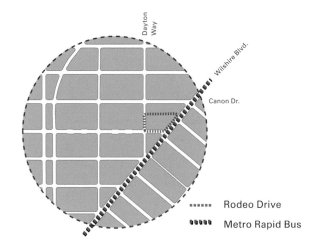

**·······** Rodeo Drive

**▪▪▪▪▪** Metro Rapid Bus

**Location Map | 1/4 mile radius** (1″ = 1/4 mile)

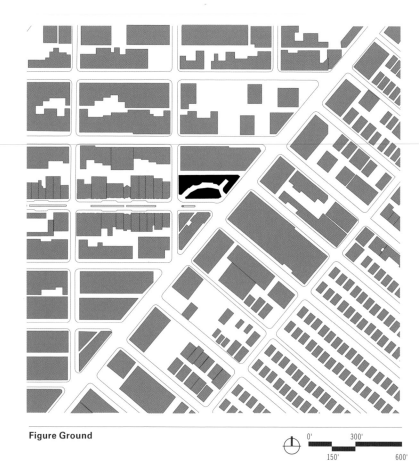

**Figure Ground**

0'    150'    300'    600'

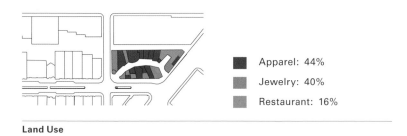

**Land Use**

■ Apparel: 44%

■ Jewelry: 40%

■ Restaurant: 16%

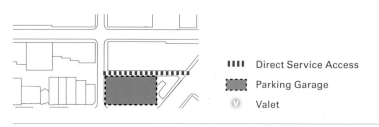

**Parking and Servicing**

**IIII** Direct Service Access

▨ Parking Garage

Ⓥ Valet

| PLAZA | AREA | LENGTH | WIDTH | IMAGES |
|---|---|---|---|---|
| dimensions | 11,000 ± square feet | 340' ± | 30' ± (ranges from 22' to 32') | |

| GROUND TREATMENT | DESIGN | AREA | AREA BREAKDOWN | |
|---|---|---|---|---|
| sidewalk paving | 1' x 1' scoring pattern (6' wide typical) | 4,000 ± square feet | 36% | |
| alley paving | 3" x 3" fan pattern (12' curb-to-curb typical) | 7,000 ± square feet | 54% | |

| TREES | QUANTITY | SPACING | LOCATION | PLANTING CONDITION |
|---|---|---|---|---|
| italian cypress (cupressus sempervirens) | 9 | 20' on center, typical | situated around seating | 6' x 6' planters |
| small planted palms | 3 | . | aligning alley | 3' diameter planters |
| royal palms (roystonea) | 15 | 30' on center, typical | along rodeo and dayton | 4' x 4' curbside beds |
| total | 23 | | | total planting ratio: 1/600± square feet |

stone pavers

| LIGHTING | QUANTITY | SPACING | LOCATION | |
|---|---|---|---|---|
| pedestrian-scale lamps | 11 | 33' on center, typical | 9"* on center, typical | |

| SEATING | QUANTITY | LOCATION | RATIO |
|---|---|---|---|
| benches | 12 | grouped at center of alley | 1/1,150 ± square feet |
| restaurant dining | 26 (tables for 2 & 4) | restaurant patio | 1,300 ± square feet (9% of total plaza area) |

landscape feature

fountain

**\*Dimension from Back of Curb**

# PLAN AND SECTION

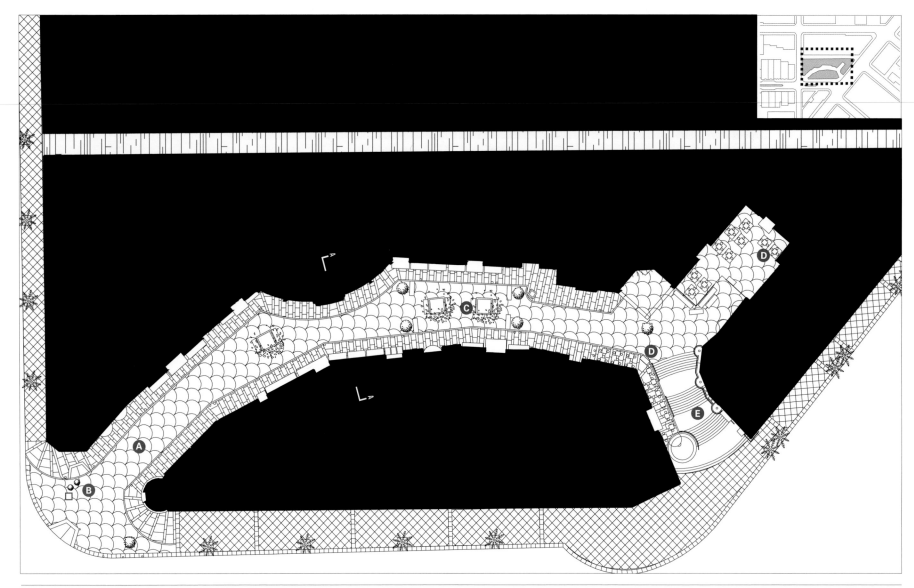

**Plaza Plan** – Via Rodeo

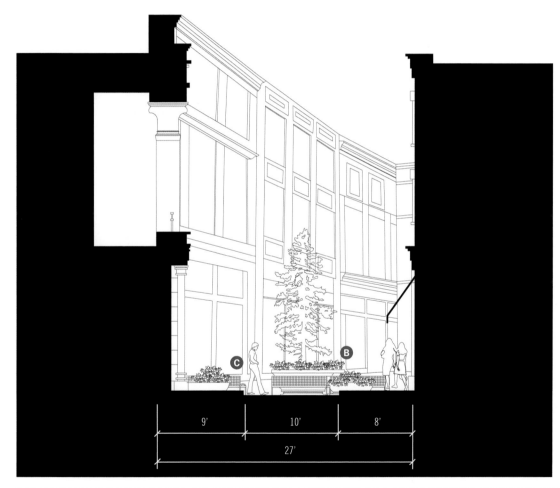

**Plaza Section AA** – Via Rodeo

A Pedestrian Passage

B Wayfinding Signage

C Seating Area

D Outdoor Dining

E Fountain / Steps

# SUMMARY FINDINGS

### Flexible Plan

Places are generally designed very simply, with an "outer ring" and an "inner ring." The outer ring accommodates a variety of activities specific to nearby businesses and buildings, and the inner ring contains a flat or terraced area that accommodates small, special events within it.

### District Appeal/Synergy of Use

The design of places and passages should respond directly to the needs of the uses that surround the space. Activities that appeal to the surrounding district can turn the plaza, place, or passage into a highly choreographed and effective community gathering place.

### Level Changes

Level changes are one way to define different activity areas around a central space, but they should maintain broad lines of sight that expand the experience to adjoining areas.

### Outdoor Dining

Informal dining is often best accommodated by outdoor seating areas that are level with the sidewalk. Permanent or temporary waist-high seating enclosures work well to differentiate walking and dining areas. Formal dining needs a higher level of separation from walking areas, which can be achieved by creating either a more private enclosed area that adjoins the public space or a raised dining terrace with views into more public activity spaces beyond.

### Landscape Approach

Because of the small scale of places, landscape treatments in them tend to emphasize simplicity and flexibility. Planters tend to follow two categories: ground-level planters with bench or flexible seating, and raised planters that incorporate seating within their design. Similarly, canopy trees tend to either ring the space or punctuate it in a cluster as a primary focal point. (For example, The Grove has specimen trees that provide shade surrounding the central space of the main plaza. Alternatively, Via Rodeo has trees that are the focal point to the space at midpassage.)

# CONCLUSION
## Essential Elements of Sustainable Urbanism

In 1900, the global population that lived in or near cities was about 13 percent. By 2050, that number is projected to rise to 70 percent. The implications of this statistic are immense for the planning profession. What tools do we have to evaluate and shape this amount of change? How can we help create a more intelligently conceived, more sustainable, and more livable city of the future?

Essential Elements of Sustainable Urbanism

After compiling information on more than 100 notable examples of urban districts from around the United States and Canada, the diversity of design solutions represents the variety of the subject matter. In comparing these examples, we have documented many obvious and distinct differences among them. The most obvious include: mix of uses, integration of transit, character of open spaces, and regional design influences. However, it's also important to note the commonalities among the projects. These make up what we think are the essential elements of sustainable urbanism:

### 1. Urbanism Is a Brand

All of the examples had a unique holistic approach to the district that informed all primary decisions. In terms of leadership, these districts are almost always proactively managed, whether by a business improvement district (BID), redevelopment agency, or the mayor's office. In the most successful examples, these managers know how to position the district in relation to other urban districts in and around the region, state, and nation. Further, the urban "brand" should inform all primary design decisions including buildings, entries, ground-floor uses, sidewalks, and public spaces. Common to the urban brand is a strong understanding of how space is layered from public to private, with strong and logical transitions.

### 2. Historic Conservation

Because urban districts are often within or adjacent to some of the most cherished parts of the city, how historical structures are incorporated into their fabric is an important element of their success. This can include setting historic structures aside as cultural artifacts; however, in North America, where historic structures are generally less old, historic buildings are often most successful when adaptively reused as part a district-wide redevelopment strategy. "Like" uses within the historic structures (commercial uses within commercial buildings) are preferable.

### 3. Legibility / Compactness

Urban districts have a scale and scope that is understandable and defined. Often, the limits of an urban district are defined by reasonable walking distances (a five-minute walking radius defines an area of roughly 160 square acres or less), with the most urban areas of a city a series of linked neighborhoods, each with a defined boundary, core, and circulation network. As a rule, a minimum gross FAR (density of buildings calculated against overall land area) of 0.75 will sustain pedestrian activity, and vital urbanism has been sustained with a gross FAR as high as 4. Significant mitigating factors such as air and water quality, noise, and access to open space begin to adversely affect the sustainability of urban districts above this density but can be overcome through thoughtful, integrated design strategy.

### 4. Targeted, Complementary Partnerships

Urban districts, through their management, seek out key players with whom they collaborate on augmenting the functional and cultural relevance of the district to residents, workers, and tourists. Recent partnerships within sustainable urban districts have focused upon attracting amenities such as service retail, hotels and entertainment, culture, and improved transit service. For example, a recent project provided a grocery store within downtown Los Angeles for the first time since the 1920s. This single use is a linchpin to the success of downtown that the city specifically targeted through cash incentives and expedited approvals. The result has been a groundswell in the number of residential units being approved and built within downtown Los Angeles. The right partners can help to make the district more convenient, vital, and integral to the life of the city.

## 5. Diversity of Uses

Social diversity is important to the life of the urban district as the hub for the exchange of ideas and cultures. The composition of land uses within the district is one of the most powerful strategic tools toward achieving this goal. This concept both applies to the types of land uses which an urban district contains (the most common mixture is residential, office, and retail, but it should also include at least one or more other uses such as hotel, civic, educational, or entertainment) and to the variety of product offerings within each land-use type. For example, within residential there should be a mix of for-sale and rental, within office a mix of "class A" and creative, within retail a mix of anchors and local shops.

## 6. Smart Infrastructure

In urban districts, the public right-of-way is designed and used by the community in a meaningful way. Streets and sidewalks are designed to accommodate a wide number of activities within a relatively narrow area. For example, streets often accommodate a variety of modes beyond automobiles—buses, light rail, bicycles, and even subways below grade. On-street parking lanes are often used as right-of-way for travel lanes during rush hour, then transferred back to on-street parking during off-peak times. Sidewalks, similarly, are optimized to accommodate a variety of activities through the day. As such, "zoning" the sidewalks for window shopping and dining, strolling, and street infrastructure is important. Canopy shade is essential to good pedestrian areas. Tree-lined streets and trellised areas help to reduce the ambient temperature, reduce glare, and improve drainage. Parking meters can help to pay for BID initiatives such as street cleaning, events, and storefront improvement programs. WiFi access, seating areas, newsstands, bike racks, public bathrooms, and information kiosks are other important amenities. All of these elements are incorporated with the intention of making the sidewalks not just pedestrian movement areas but a "third place" for social interaction.

## 7. Learning and Contemplation

Continuing education is an essential factor in the ability to compete in the 21st century. To that end, urban districts should provide the armature that can facilitate education—libraries, college "satellite" campuses, language and computer classes, and access to conference convention facilities are all essential to regional competition in a global marketplace, which should be located within urban districts. At the same time, life cannot be just about competition. Areas for thought and contemplation are important to maintain life balance and manage stress. A network of formal and informal areas for rest and worship are also important to the functioning urban district.

8. Events and Entertainment

One of the most important elements of the urban district is spectacle and circumstance—unique experiences that only urban districts can provide. We guess events are part of the "there" that Gertrude Stein referred to in her famous quote. Formal event venues such as ballparks, arenas, or theatres with events programmed throughout the year, nightclubs and bars with live entertainment, formal scheduled outdoor events such as theatre and movies in the park, farmers markets and other seasonal events, and, finally, informal "impromptu" experiences such as street vendors and performers. These experiences reinforce the primacy of the street as the public forum and define the urban district as a unique venue in the city.

What Is Next?

Cities are part of a regional ecosystem. Research will continue to be a tool that is vital to inform the planning, design, and development of urban areas. However, we are just beginning to understand the fundamental linkages between our various, often conflicting development aspirations. Our diversity, market-based orientation, and traditionally laissez-faire attitudes toward planning have forced American cities to overemphasize competition for markets and resources and underemphasize a more systemic, regional approach where natural, cultivated, semi-urban, and urban areas are stewarded as part of a whole. The results over the last 25 years have been inconsistent: the renaissance of some areas has often been offset by social inequities and enviromental degradations in others. Only time will tell as to whether we can start thinking with greater regard for a more systemic sustainable urbanism.

# INDEX

# ABOUT THE AUTHOR

Nathan Cherry, AICP, is vice president of RTKL Associates. With more than 20 years of experience as an architect and urban designer, he specializes in large urban infill and brownfield redevelopments, transit-oriented development, and sports and entertainment districts. He has extensive experience working throughout the western United States, Hawaii, Canada, Asia, Russia, and Australia. He has been lead designer on numerous award-winning projects, including the Los Angeles Sports and Entertainment District, Downtown Brea Redevelopment, the Pasadena Central District Specific Plan, and Tustin Legacy. He is on retainer as town architect for numerous municipalities in Southern California.